IDEAS IN
WEAVING

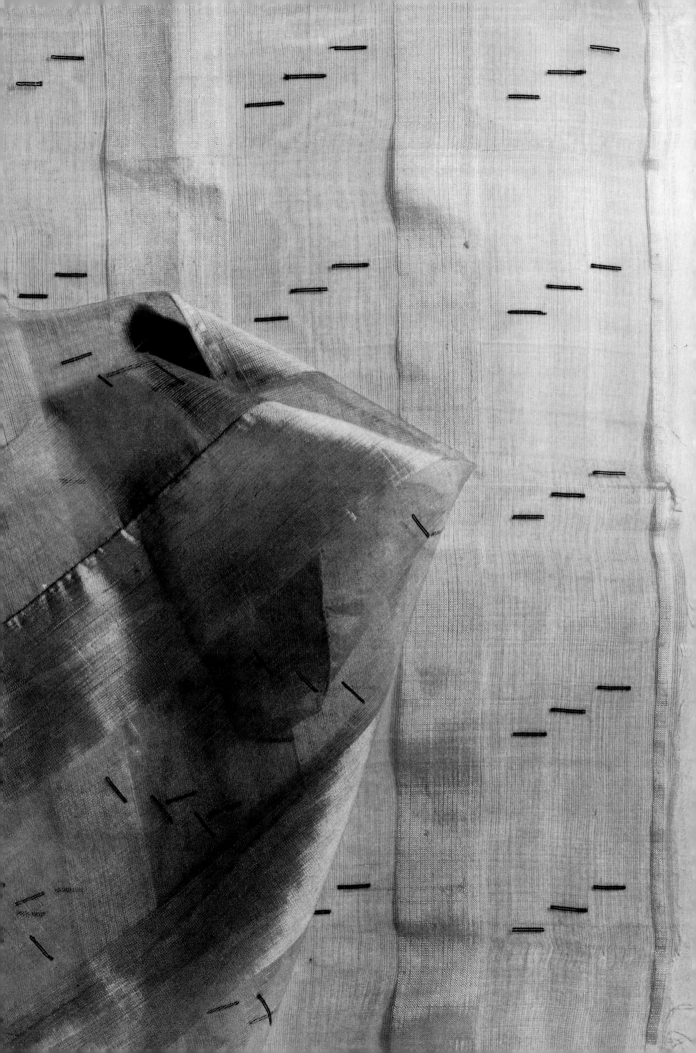

IDEAS IN
WEAVING

Ann Sutton and Diane Sheehan
Photography by David Cripps

INTERWEAVE PRESS
Loveland, Colorado, U.S.A

CONTENTS

To Lottie

INTERWEAVE PRESS, Inc.
306 North Washington Avenue
Loveland, Colorado 80537, U.S.A.

Copyright © Ann Sutton and Diane Sheehan 1989
Photographs Copyright © Bellew Publishing Co. Ltd 1989

Designed and produced by
BELLEW PUBLISHING COMPANY LTD
7 Southampton Place, London WC1A 2DR

Library of Congress Cataloging in Publication Data

Sutton, Ann
    Ideas in weaving/Ann Sutton and Diane Sheehan:
    photography by David Cripps.

    p.   cm.
    Bibilography: p.
    Includes index.
    ISBN 0-934026-42-4 : $29.95
    1. Hand weaving   I. Sheehan, Diane. II. Title.
TT848.S885   1988
746.1'4--dc19

Designed by Michael Head
Diagrams by Ethan Danielson

Printed in Italy by New Interlitho S.p.A. − Milan

Jacket illustration:
Double-cloth fabric: when relaxed after weaving, the
cotton areas 'blister' due to the elasticity of high twist
polyester in the other layer (Junichi Arai: Japan)

Frontispiece:
Piña fibre cloth. Philippines, early 20th century.
(Larry Edman Collection)

Contents:
Warp-printed silk ribbon. French, c.1900.
(Larry Edman Collection)

INTRODUCTION

Man should be prouder of having invented the hammer
and nail than of having created masterpieces of imitation.
— Hegel

This book, a logical sequel to *The Structure of Weaving*, is
for everyone who makes, uses and appreciates beautifully
designed and executed cloth. It is assumed that the reader
has basic knowledge of the process of weaving and
shaft-controlled weaves. The possibilities for excitement in
these textiles is vast: inventions and combinations of
materials and techniques have fascinated weavers since cloth
was first woven, and they are seemingly inexhaustible. The
imagery found in other types of weaving such as Jacquard
and tapestry is rarely integrated with the process and
structure and therefore is outside the range of this book,
although sometimes an example is included to illustrate
another aspect of the fabric.

By beginning with the topics of creativity, thinking and
planning we hope to point out that these are the most
important and usually the most neglected aspects of the
production of ingenious cloth. Weavers tend to see
themselves as doers, and indeed much time is needed to do
weaving – but much time is wasted as well. Considering
those aspects of creative thinking which are peculiar to cloth
design might serve to distinguish weavers from those artists
and makers who choose other media.

The largest section of this book is a compendium of ideas
and innovations that have made possible the impossible in
woven cloth. Some of these processes are historical, some
contemporary, some are industrial, some primitive. All
produce cloths with built-in structural integrity, more
satisfying than the effects of superficially applied design and
pattern. A chronological history of these inventions has not
been the aim. The history of such processes is as difficult to
sort out as textile terms and definitions (even between two
English-speaking countries). Our goal of encouraging the
quantum leap between the genius of the past and previously
unexplored possibilities would not be served by lists of dates
and attributions. Neither does the text suggest specific end
uses for these processes. Functional and Fine Art weaving are
on an equal footing here. The pursuit of quality in thought
and in result is paramount.

FOREWORD

From ancient times to the present day, mankind has been deeply concerned with fabric, from the cloth we are wrapped in at birth to the cloth we are wrapped in at death. If people were naked they would be like animals. By wearing fabric, we become aware of the changing weather and of sensations on the skin; we also derive feelings of joy and sadness from our clothing. Fabric clothes not only the body, but also the spirit. Clothes are the proud emblem that connects us to God, and the weaver is a standard-bearer. Weavers were the standard-bearers for both the Renaissance and the Industrial Revolution.

Thus, the present technological world began from the relationship of people to fabric. And if we can properly understand both the advantages and the pitfalls of new technology, we can start to make truly contemporary fabric. When things are made which look only backwards, to the supposedly golden past, they are the products of the nostalgia of weak people. Making a contemporary weave is like planting a seed into a new, uncultivated field. When the seed sprouts, the resulting fabric is a fruit which communicates with all our senses and makes us rejoice.

Newly conceived fabrics change our consciousness, change our spirit and so can change future society. This, therefore, is the mission of the weaver today: to pose the

challenge of a new human revolution. Weaver! You are carrying the responsibility of beauty! What will you say if you cannot say, 'this is a weaver's honour'?

A poet cannot write a poem if he has no words. In the same way, a contemporary weaver cannot create cloth without ideas. We cannot fulfil the needs of people today by mere nostalgia. We must understand the desires of the modern spirit so that we can create a truly appropriate contemporary fabric.

Creating an image is the first step in making a work of art. But image alone cannot produce fabric; we need much more basic information in order to start to create: fibre, colour and twist of thread, weave structure, sett and possible effect of finishing. We cannot start to create without our experience being applied to this information. But selecting from the possibilities offered by this information is essentially an ability of the soul. Fine contemporary cloths are the results of the human spirit and new technology working hand in hand.

We are asked about the ability of our soul to make such selections. The most enjoyable part of a weaver's task is transforming an idea into cloth. If a poet has only a limited amount of inspiration, he flounders: similarly, weavers must do more thinking and develop their ideas. Fortunately,

the contemporary weaver has much new technology at his disposal, but this is also his greatest misfortune. He is confused and afraid of the tool that is the computer. This can only lead into a labyrinth with no exit.

How do we create ideas? How do we become inspired and cultivate the wasteland? The answer lies in the ability of the spirit to create and to nurture.

Junichi Arai

Junichi Arai, Hon R.D.I.

This magenta/black scarf designed by Junichi Arai has a fine cotton warp. The magenta cloth has a high twist wool weft interspersed with polyurethane yarn (one pick in three). Their stretch properties condense that cloth, making the black one (2-fold wool weft) fold and crinkle. This is controlled into pleats by the removal of some warp threads in the same place on both top and bottom layers: the energy of the high-twist yarns is released along those lines, making the scarf pleat and fold.

JUNICHI ARAI
IN PERSPECTIVE

... craft has three historical stages. First there is the time when everything is craft. All processes of making are hand processes, everything made, whether utilitarian, ritual or merely decorative (and often one cannot separate these functions), is essentially a craft object. Later, at least in Europe, from the Renaissance onwards, it is possible to distinguish two further stages of development. There was an intellectual separation between the idea of craft and that of fine art, which eventually came to be regarded as superior. This development is one of the distinguishing marks of the European Renaissance. Later still with the Industrial Revolution, there arrived a separation between a craft object and the thing made by a machine − an industrial product. − Edward Lucie-Smith, *The Story of Craft*

Despite the protests of William Morris and John Ruskin, the machines that transformed an ancient craft, based on the seasonal rhythms of rustic living, into the production-oriented, factory-based urban nightmare of the Industrial Revolution, are now being domesticated and re-evaluated by a new craft community. Sophisticated weavers recognize the computer and the production loom as having the potential to work for, rather than against, the creative artist. It can be considered that it wasn't the machine that led to the decline of quality, design and innovation, but the separation of the person who thinks about weaving from the person who weaves. The sheer scale of mass production that the machines made possible also had a deleterious effect.

A new, more harmonious relationship is possible between the mind, the hand and the machine in our present climate of small business and appreciation of quality over quantity.

Junichi Arai serves as the model of the kind of philosophical, intellectual and technological synthesis that is now possible. His work recaptures the admiration we feel for the cloths so miraculously produced by the primitive looms of Pre-Columbian Peru, though it is emphatically a product of our contemporary global culture, using all the high-tech available to produce sumptuous fabrics.

1 Double-cloth in cotton. Central Coast, Peru, c.1200-1400 A.D.
2 Kimono fabric in overspun silk, kasuri patterned in warp and weft. Japan, possibly late 19th century.
3 Warp seersucker in overspun and regular yarns. Silk shawl, 19th century.

3

2

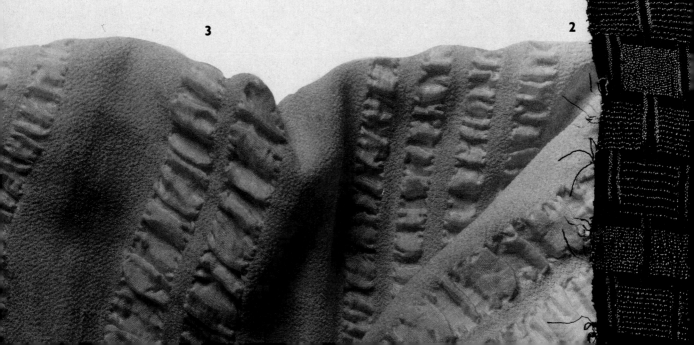

I

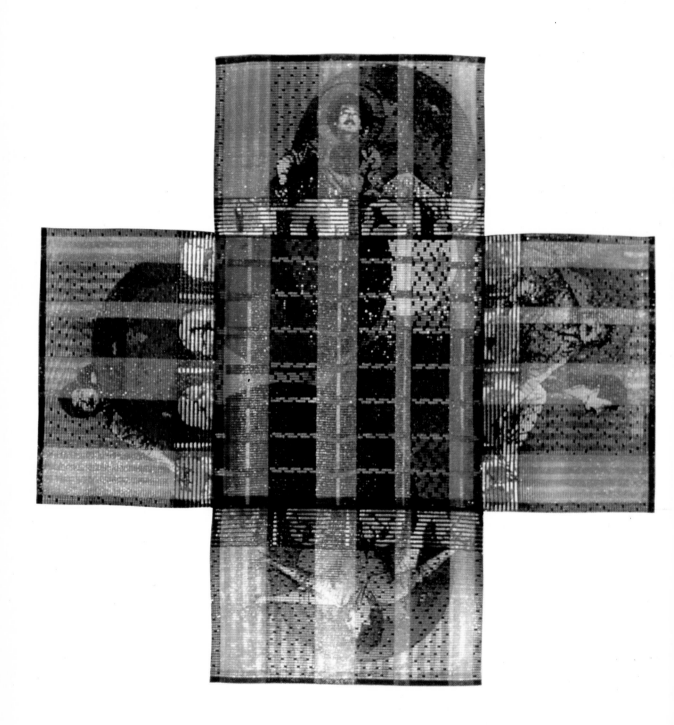

12

1. CREATIVITY

The word 'creativity', like the word 'weaving', is often used and seldom really thought about. We know that they are both activities basic to civilization, but most people are oblivious of what brings them about: creativity being too mysterious to think about and weaving too mundane. Many great leaps (creative breakthroughs) in technology have been associated with the production of cloth. The history of innovation within the textile industry can serve as a map of human inventiveness. Although a plain woven cloth would suffice for almost every human need, fascination with its possibilities has led to a passion for both structural and poetic invention.

On the following pages, modes of creative thinking used in many fields of human endeavour will be discussed as an encouragement to focus on, rethink and reinvent the woven textile.

Left:
Gerhardt Knodel (USA): 'Guardians of the New Day',
7 ft × 7 ft (213 cm × 213 cm), 1987. (Photo by the artist)

CHALLENGING THE COMMONPLACE

What we know too well, rather than what we don't know, is often the greatest deterrent to creative thinking. (Trees are green with brown trunks, shoes have openings for feet, baskets are made of long fibres woven or bound together.)

Since fabrics pervade our environment and fabric designers are trained on pattern books and heavy doses of textile history, preconceptions about weaving are perhaps the most difficult to overcome. Breaking the cycle of assumptions about the loom, the process of weaving and the inherent nature of cloth requires a healthy scepticism, an irreverent attitude towards the 'rules' of weaving and a fresh, unfettered vision.

According to the psychologist Carl R. Rogers in 'Toward a Theory of Creativity' (in *The Creativity Question,* edited by Albert Rothenberg and Carl Hausman), there are three characteristics a creative person must have: an openness to, and an awareness of experience; a self-reliant, independent

approach to finding solutions; and a flexible, even playful attitude towards manipulating concepts and ideas.

Issey Miyake and John McQueen have each taken a fresh look at commonplace objects, transforming them into witty sculptural forms that satisfy on many levels from the desire for pure function to the philosophical implications of shoes that can lock out the wearer or a basket too prickly to be touched. These objects exist in some realm outside the categories of 'art', 'craft' or 'design'; their scope is too large for mere labels.

Left:
Issey Miyake (Japan): Shoes with zipped opening. (Photo by Ann Sutton. Hiroko Pijanowski Collection)

Below:
John McQueen (USA): Untitled. Basket of burrs, 21 in × 12 in × 12 in (53 cm × 31 cm × 31 cm), 1987. Detail of same. (Photos by the artist)

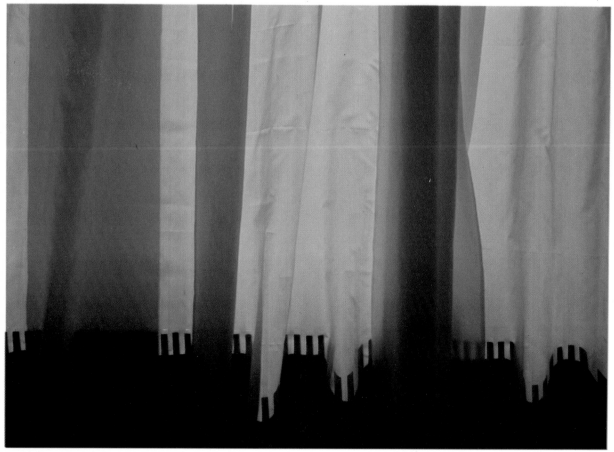

SEEING IN NEW WAYS

Much of the satisfaction that art offers lies in its ability to make us see the world we have always known in a completely new way: making the strange seem familiar and the familiar seem strange. What we consider 'familiar' is based on our past experience. If our experience is limited or our knowledge incorrect, we may live in a world of illusion. Although some people prefer not to be jolted into new ways of experiencing, creative people crave and thrive on ideas which change for ever their previous notions.

For textile designers, completely new problems, materials or techniques seldom arise. The challenge is to see old problems and processes in new ways. Surveying previous ingenious inventions and solutions is the intent of this book, but the examples put forth here will succeed only if readers of unique vision see new ways of using them.

In Western culture fabrics have been seen in rather limited ways: either as a relatively unobtrusive but necessary part of the environment, or perhaps as imitation paintings, as in pictorial tapestries. Here we show two images which transform fabric into enigma and metaphor, giving it the power of mystery and expression. The image above left is actually fabric performing its most mundane function as 'rag', but it manages to shield and protect nature as reflected in the mirror with heroic humility. The plainest white woven fabric, when set in motion by a breeze at an open window, folding and unfolding, diffuses light in constantly changing compositions. Here it becomes apparent that even in the simplest cloth, choice of fibre type and size, sett of weave and ultimate transparency and drapability are all monumental decisions which bear heavily on the effect of the finished fabric.

Above left:
'Mirror in Barcelona', 1981. (Photo by John Markley)

Left: 'Curtain and radiator'. (Photo by Diane Sheehan)

HUMAN STATUE OF LIBERTY
18,000 OFFICERS AND MEN
AT
CAMP DODGE, DES MOINES IA.
COL. WM. NEWMAN, COMMANDING
COL. RUSH S. WELLS, DIRECTING.

MOLE & THOMAS
915 MEDINAH BLDG.
CHICAGO, ILL.

18

CREATING ORDER OUT OF CHAOS

In the solving of problems and in the creation of physical forms the driving force is a craving for unity and order. There is a natural desire to orchestrate ideas and visual elements into a meaningful whole.

This concept is obvious to weavers who spend so much time and energy coaxing unruly threads into order. In fact, it may be one of the most attractive aspects of the process. While stereotyped thinkers will work with the most obvious plan, creative pattern seekers will delve into alternative solutions through the use of what Edward de Bono termed 'lateral thinking'. This means considering a number of possible alternatives, turning the problem over and inside out mentally, perhaps even manipulating objects physically (fiddling or sampling) before proceeding to the solution.

The pictures on these pages stretch our notion of what constitutes legitimate image-making materials. In 1918 the photographers Arthur S. Mole and John D. Thomas organized 18,000 officers and men into the Human Statue of Liberty, managing to create the illusion of a figure parallel with the picture plane while in fact it recedes some miles into the distance. While technically astounding, the image is even more powerful for the spirit of patriotism and devotion to communal values that it embodies. The sculptor Andy Goldsworthy works with nature, intuitively altering and reorganizing ephemeral colours and textures into new and surprising realities. These examples, off-beat as they are, indicate the strength and diversity of the ordering impulse: while making us realize that the medium has everything to do with the power of the message.

Above:
Andy Goldsworthy: Foxglove leaves split down centre vein laid around hole, 1977. (Photo by the artist)

Left:
'The Human Statue of Liberty'. (Photo by Arthur S. Mole and John D. Thomas. Courtesy of the Chicago Historical Society)

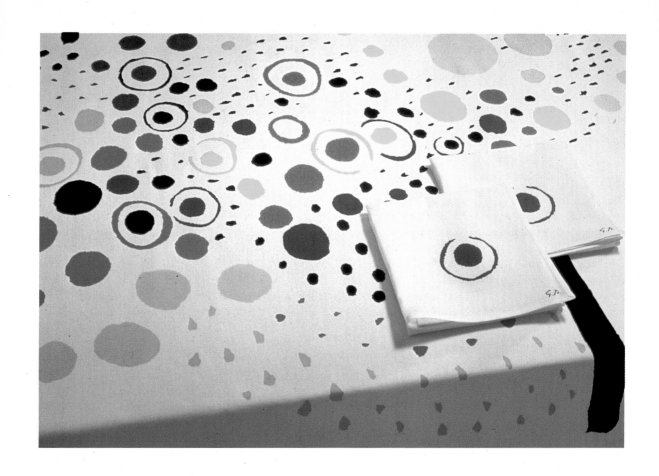

MAKING CONNECTIONS

Rather than cultivating thought patterns that seek to categorize and isolate phenomena into neat compartments, creative thinkers prefer shifting and overlapping ideas and information into flexible relationships. This kind of thinking is particularly relevant to our contemporary culture in which simultaneity of experience is a way of life. We eat and watch television, drive and listen to the radio, talk on the phone while doing all of the above. Discrete experience is really a rarity, yet the unusual juxtapositions and associations produced in the course of daily events is often lost.

Concentrating on hidden connections might enable a weaver to arrive at unexpected combinations. Realizing that double-cloth and warp-faced fabric are based on a similarly close sett would lead to cloths which make use of both these constructions; associating accidental mistakes such as unwanted shrinkage with their potential for shaping a fabric if properly controlled, would lead to garments which formed themselves in the finishing process. There need be no mistakes in weaving, only possibilities.

Sonia Delaunay's sensitivity to pulsating colour and primary forms are here used as a scheme for a table setting. Having developed an abstract style of painting through an appreciation of the beauty of quilts, Delaunay eventually came full circle back to objects of use. These printed textiles make use of energetic circular forms, characteristic of her painting style, often combined with place settings to fit perfectly into the design. They transform the table top into a work of art and celebration in which the diners can participate.

The famous Swedish textile designer Astrid Sampe became attracted to Mondrian's paintings in the late 1940s, and related his organization of line and area to warp and weft in weaving, and to the order and structure of architecture. In her design collection 'Linenline', she used this inspiration in a series of linen placemats in which the lines contained the plate and cutlery and the stable areas of colour were provided by folded napkins in primary blue, red and yellow.

Above left:
Sonia Delaunay: 'Constellation', tablecloth, 71 in × 108 in (180 cm × 275 cm). (Artcurial Collection)

Left:
Astrid Sampe's linen damask placemat 'Negroni': designed for Almedahls Fabriker AB, Sweden, 1955.

USING CHANCE

Some people cultivate and encourage associative thinking by tuning into it or provoking it. Some pay attention to dreams (a state in which there is no awareness of incongruity), others may play games in which random pairings of known facts may produce unexpected avenues for problem-solving. Patrick Gunkel has developed a new field he calls 'Ideonomy' in which he uses a computer to generate 'idea combinatorics' or unique pairings of facts on any subject. Visual artists and designers have been engaging in this kind of activity for centuries without calling it a science.

Ideas often occur through the juxtaposing of two or more thoughts which had not come together before. Even a combination which at first seems ridiculous may turn out to be an idea which, with or without modification, could become a discovery capable of sustaining many variations and subsequent development. Many of the 'ideas' in this book started as the result of a chance remark, an untried combination of techniques, or even a challenge.

It seemed that weavers needed an aid which would speed up the process of 'chance combinations', and 'The Design Game' was evolved by Ann Sutton in order to stimulate and challenge groups of weavers.

'The Design Game'

'The Design Game' is played like an open game of Pontoon (Twenty-Ones, Vingt-et-Un, Blackjack). Each card in the pack (at least 50) contains an element of design found in a woven cloth. A player is dealt two cards and is asked to read them aloud. If the elements conflict irredeemably, the dealer moves on to the next player, who might have two cards which are more amenable, and feels that a third element could be incorporated into the cloth (the vision of which builds up differently in the minds of all in the group). A fourth card could then be accepted, and even a fifth. Each should be read out and considered, with solutions suggested by the group for any 'impossibilities'. If the player accepts a card which counteracts a previous one and makes the fabric truly impossible, then the dealer declares him 'bust' and moves on to the next player.

The purpose of the game is to produce, by chance, unexpected combinations of technique, weave, colour, finishing, etc., and to create a problem-solving attitude to design challenges. It has usually been found to be a mind-stretching experience enjoyed by weavers of all abilities.

The cards should be similar to playing cards in size, and all of exactly the same size for easy shuffling. The 'elements

of design' should be typed or printed very clearly. A list of suggested elements follows. It will be found that a near-even quantity in each of seven categories will give the best results, but the cards should be mixed together and not dealt from the separate lists.

Technique
Resist dye the warp
Not more than four shafts
Make good use of two warp beams
Incorporate floats in warp and weft
Undulating twill
Use satin weave

Colour
One colour only
Use black as an outline
Close tone (value) colours only
Use bright colours on a white background
Rich, dark colours
Use shades and varieties of white only
Use different hues, same tone (value)
Use one colour, many tones (values)
Use some bright, some dark colours
Very bright colours only
Very pale colours only
Black-and-white only
Two colours only

Yarn
Make your own yarn without spinning
Ply two of the yarns together
Include a space-dyed yarn
Use some fancy yarns in warp and weft
Use two yarns of very different thickness in the warp
Include ribbon
Spin a special yarn for it
Use overspun yarn or elastic
Use some chenille
Use rag as yarn

Fibre
Use more than one fibre
Include some Lurex
Use silk
Use linen only

Use worsted-spun wool only
Use woollen yarn only
Use manmade fibres only
To be made of wool

Finishing
Beetle it
Plan it to be piece-dyed
Design the cloth to be pleated
Stitch the cloth, in squares
Include some embroidery
Stitch it boldly
Include patches or darns
Brush (raise) some or all of the cloth
Print it afterwards
Shrink it

General design
A small check
A large-scale design
Based on a traditional tweed
Sparkling
Base the design on 'patchwork'
Regular spots
Incorporate some holes
Give a diagonal emphasis
Narrow warp stripes
Striped
A small geometric pattern
A large check

Warp stripes
Base the design on 'tartan'
Base the design on a grid
To look ancient and faded
Use cut fringes in the weave
A warp-faced fabric
Some areas to be padded during weaving
Use a colour-and-weave effect
Two shafts only
Include some knitting
Incorporate beads
Include knots
Not more than six ends per inch
Weave it in narrow strips and join them together
Crammed-and-spaced in the reed
Paint or bleach the warp
Incorporate sequins
Resist-dyed weft
Transparent in parts
Weave tucks into the fabric

Weave
Incorporate areas of double-cloth
Use a large, bold herringbone
Use overshot weaves
Use twill
Combine two weaves
Include a lace-weave
Use only plain weave
Block weave

Overleaf:
Cloths which could have been designed as a result of the Chance Design game:

1 Ikat dyed warp: use leather: discontinuous weft (designed by Leonarda Capuyan, Philippines)
2 Use waffle weave; some yarn to be overspun; a shot fabric (designed by Ann Richards, West Surrey College of Art and Design, UK)
3 Use padding in the weft; warp stripes; incorporate waved lines (designed by Annabelle Aguire, West Surrey College of Art and Design, UK)

2

3

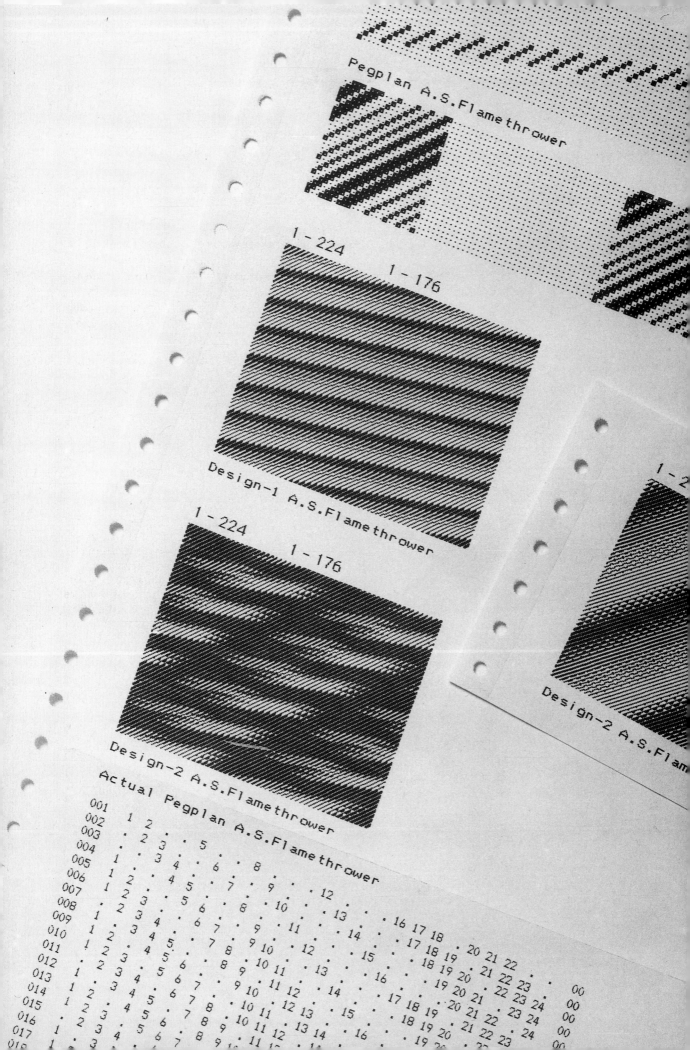

Pegplan A.S.Flamethrower

1 - 224
1 - 176

Design-1 A.S.Flamethrower

1 - 224
1 - 176

1 - 2

Design-2 A.S.Fla

Design-2 A.S.Flamethrower

Actual Pegplan A.S.Flamethrower

```
001                1   2
002            .   2   3   .   5
003        1   .   3   4   .   6   .   8
004    1   2   3   .   5   .   7   .   9   .   .  12
005    1   2   3   4   5   .   7   .   9   .   .  12   .   .   .  16  17  18   .   .  20  21  22
006    1   2   3   4   5   6   .   8   .  10   .   .  13   .   .   .   17  18  19   .  20   .  21  22  23   .      00
007    1   2   3   4   5   6   7   .   9   .  11   .   .  14   .   .   .   17  18  19   20   .  21   .  22  23  24   00
008    1   2   3   4   5   6   7   8   .  10   .   .  13   .   15   .   .   .   19  20   21   .  22   .  23  24   00
009    1   2   3   4   5   6   7   8   9   10  11   .  13   .   .  16   .   .   .   19  20  21   .  22   .  23  24   00
010    1   2   3   4   5   6   7   8   9   10  11  12  13   .   15   .   .   18  19  20   21   .  22  23   24   00
011    1   2   3   4   5   6   7   8   9   10  11  12  13  14   .   16   .   .   18  19  20   21   .  22  23   24   00
```

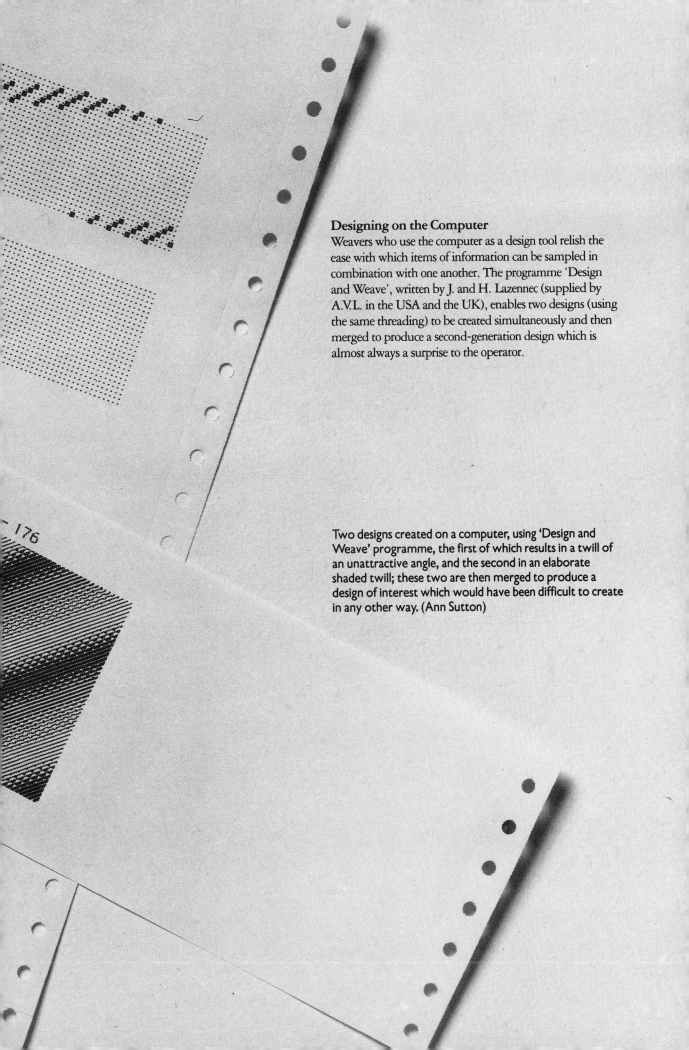

Designing on the Computer

Weavers who use the computer as a design tool relish the ease with which items of information can be sampled in combination with one another. The programme 'Design and Weave', written by J. and H. Lazennec (supplied by A.V.L. in the USA and the UK), enables two designs (using the same threading) to be created simultaneously and then merged to produce a second-generation design which is almost always a surprise to the operator.

Two designs created on a computer, using 'Design and Weave' programme, the first of which results in a twill of an unattractive angle, and the second in an elaborate shaded twill; these two are then merged to produce a design of interest which would have been difficult to create in any other way. (Ann Sutton)

TAKING RISKS

Playing safe has never produced exciting cloth. Any historical study of textiles reveals that weavers in the past were often much more adventurous with their fabric than weavers of today. Handweavers are notorious for a nervous attitude towards cutting their cloth into shaped garments, as if every cut will produce irrevocable fraying. They are nervous of most 'finishing' even while realizing that most cloths are incomplete without it. Yet the very act which is potentially ruinous to the fabric can transform it from a run-of-the-mill item to a thing of trembling beauty, as if a reward for the risk which was taken.

Square shawl, Jacquard woven, in black silk and gold thread. The coloured areas are discharged of their black dye and printed with colour – neither of these processes will affect the gold weft. Probably French, c.1920.

COMMUNICATING

Weavers, like most other creative people, may dream of peace and total isolation, but few are capable of generating ideas in such conditions. When at college, art and design students are constantly generating new ideas, encouraged by the proximity and competition of other students and by the expectations of the faculty. On leaving this environment, most are unable to maintain this level of creativity, unless they work in a design studio where such an atmosphere is consciously maintained. Weavers who are working in other circumstances look to different sources for creative stimulation, often in the form of regular or occasional attendance at teaching workshops, or the short, sharp blast of a conference. It is sometimes not realized that, at these meetings, the interchange of ideas is as important as the officially scheduled 'learning'. The value of the 'extra-curricular input' over coffees, lunches and in social periods is recognized by organizers of industrial training programmes.

Specialist workshops in weaving are often attended by weavers who have fixed ideas of what they wish to achieve. A more relaxed approach to learning will always achieve more, even if in unexpected directions, than a rigid, blinkered attitude. Like the game of 'Chinese Whispers', *misunderstanding* the lecturer can often lead to more creativity than full comprehension.

Some weavers communicate by post: Sherri Smith (USA) had the idea of a package of 'slides', information and samples constantly circulating among a number of weavers, each of whom would update their personal contribution before sending it on. Sheila Hicks (USA and France) produced fold-up broadsheets of textile news and thoughts, even crosswords, called 'Buttonhole' (referring to the need to grab the attention of the reader, in textile terms).

Other communication may be for the purpose of selling work. This is currently one of the most researched fields of communication, but there is still room for creativity and original thinking in the way in which one person tells another about his or her product.

A weaver can often convey an idea of current work by a postage stamp-sized clipping of actual cloth incorporated into the design of a business card or letterhead. Tiny adhesive colour photographs can be used in the same way. The American weaver Randall Darwall had the idea of creating small 'treasure boxes' of little bunches of silk threads (from thrums), tiny clippings of cloth, a seedhead, or pebble, or whatever conveyed the colour feeling of his next collection, and sent them as informative reminders to his customers, many of whom would be anxious to add to their collection of his scarves. These inventive solutions are welcomed by the recipient: very few are thrown away, so communication is successful.

Developments in Communication

With the new technology, communication problems are being solved daily in ingenious and fantastic ways. While it is generally recognized that computer-aided design is probably more compatible with weaving than with any other craft or design area, weavers have been slower to realize the potential of other modern tools increasingly available to most people, which can help both design and communication.

The **photocopier** will produce an instant, cheap, same-sized image of any piece of cloth. Often this image, perhaps combined with a bunch of the yarns used, will be sufficient to inform a potential purchaser.

It can also be used as a way of trying out colours (painting on the photocopy), or testing different proportions (cutting up the image and reassembling; perhaps photocopying the result). If a copier is available which will reduce or magnify, it will be possible to see the appearance of the sample in different scales. Some of the more recent copiers give excellent images of even the subtlest cloths, and some are able to copy in colour.

The **fax** machine can transmit a photocopy of a fabric to the other side of the world, to be received by a similar machine within seconds. This visual information is sent by telephone, and the original image is retained by the sender. This makes it possible for weavers on different continents to develop an idea jointly, with constant and instant communication.

Warp-dyed silk scarf, cut float weave, by Randall Darwall (USA), with presentation box and leaflet.

DESCRIPTION:

FIBER CONTENT:

SILK

combined with
MOHAIR
WOOL
METALLIC
RAYON
COTTON
LINEN
OTHER:

80%

20%

RANDALL DARWAI

2. PRE-WEAVING

THINKING ABOUT WEAVING

An awareness of thought processes and problem-solving strategies is the most important lesson students can learn. These are not ends in themselves but, like learning to ride a bicycle, they will eventually make the journey possible without being preoccupied with the means of conveyance. Some will protest that artistic activity cannot be subjected to methodical analysis, that it is ephemeral and beyond the reach of logic. This is partly true. There is no way to describe exactly what happens at that moment when the bicycle doesn't fall over: all the psycho-motor operations that come into play are impossible to explain to the learner. What is experienced is the miracle of something that seemed impossible becoming not only possible, but easy.

We might divide the world into two schools of thought: Classical, which relies on logic and order; and Romantic, which relies on intuition and emotion. In fact we normally operate somewhere on a sliding scale between these two extremes, using our intellect and involvement in the physical world, tempered by the feelings and dreams of the subconscious. The manifestations of these two modes of operation (the art, literature, science produced) can also be referred to as classical and romantic in form (although in this instance we are not necessarily referring to specific periods such as late eighteenth-century European Romanticism in art and literature).

It could be argued that all woven works require a classical approach, and that all weavers must have a natural affinity for logic, order, tradition and restraint. The more romantic, creative types have long since abandoned the constraints of the loom for less structured methods of making. The real difference between weaving and painting may not be an argument of 'craft' vs 'art' but a preference for classicism over romanticism. Although we have examples of weavers who have tried to press the loom into producing highly organic and emotional works which deny the very structure and order of warp and weft, most have found better, certainly more efficient, ways of producing these effects, using other techniques.

1 Shirting material, cotton. (Amanda Spencer, West Surrey College of Art and Design, UK)
2 Silk warp, metallic weft. Jacquard, printed after weaving. Probably French, late 19th century.

2

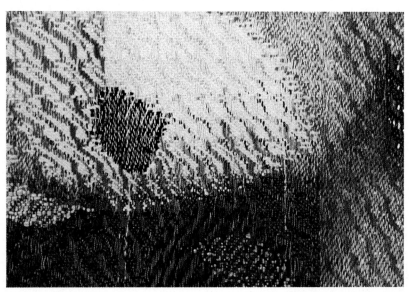

It should not be assumed that because fabric-making is essentially classical in both intellectual and physical processes, that fabrics cannot be expressive. Every maker is bound by the initial choice of a medium to work within its constraints (perhaps pushing it to the limit) while producing work of individuality which tells something of the maker's point of view. Edgar Allen Poe first decided that writing would be his work, then decided on the **form** (novel or poem) the work would take and then decided on the **effect** he wanted to achieve. Every subsequent decision was based on the best way to achieve that effect. (See Poe's essay 'Creation as Craft' in *The Creativity Question,* edited by Albert Rothenberg and Carl R. Hausman.)

The rules of weaving are no less rigorous than the rules of language. The same range of difference exists between textbook writing (descriptive, didactic) and poetry (emotive, original) as between serviceable cloth and magical cloth. Issey Miyake is said to have asked Junichi Arai to make fabrics evocative of other substances or of emotional states ('make me a fabric like poison') as a means of inspiration. The discipline of adhering to the structure and order of weaving while imagining the unseen sets up a tension in the designer and in the finished cloth that is the basis of its power.

Left:
Cynthia Schira (USA): 'Winter Dream', 60 in × 65 in (152 cm × 165 cm), 1986. (Spencer Art Museum, University of Kansas, Collection)

Below left:
Detail of above

Below:
Emma Osbourn (West Surrey College of Art and Design, UK): 'Landscape', 5 in × 6.5 in (13 cm × 17 cm).

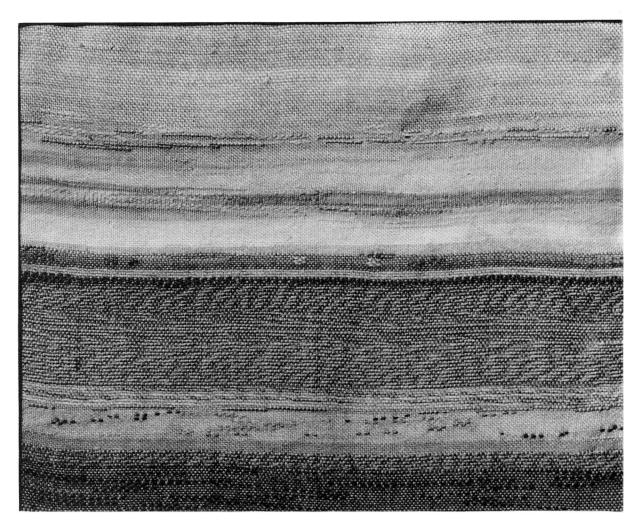

Time is a greater factor in cloth-making than most weavers realize. That weaving is a time-consuming activity has not escaped anyone, but the effect that time has on how we think and work deserves some attention. First, weaving progresses step by step (weft by weft) and going back to make changes or repair mistakes is excruciating. One can compare this line-building in weaving to the way writers or composers work, if one eliminates the possibility of deleting and revising. Instead of starting at the top and working our way to the bottom (as our brains have loved to do since we first were applauded for learning to read), we must weave from the bottom up. This may not pose a problem to weavers of patterns, but where any sense of composition comes into play, it requires thinking in a new way. Whereas cloth is constructed in a sequential manner, the structure and the design are built in simultaneously: they are the same. This is a unique and complex phenomenon.

Since reworking a cloth is out of the question, and since most of it is out of view during the process of weaving, pre-planning and the ability to visualize the product before the first pick is woven — before the warp is even measured — is essential. More than any other process, weaving requires a commitment to planning, repetition and geometry. Enjoying the challenge of these constraints distinguishes the weaver. The problems posed become games and puzzles to be manipulated and resolved.

Peruvian weavers, needing to weave larger cloths than their arm span allowed on the back-strap loom, probably devised a method of weaving multi-layered cloths folded accordion fashion on the loom. We have specimens of cloths up to 14 ft 7 in. wide, but no evidence of looms wide enough to have woven them. Peruvian weavers used multi-layered cloths for both decorative (as in double-weave pick-up designs) and utilitarian (as in double-strength carrying straps) purposes. It would certainly not have been beyond the scope of the Pre-Columbian weaver to have made the giant leap between what was known and what was needed.

1 Double cloth wool scarf, based on Russian Constructivist design. (Junichi Arai, Japan)
2 Double cloth with supplementary weft-faced dots. Pre-Columbian Peru, Central Coast. (Larry Edman Collection)

2

PLANNING

In other words, to locate a star involves the checking of various maps against the vault of the sky, with all the related actions: putting on and taking off eyeglasses, turning the flashlight on and off, unfolding and folding the large chart, losing and finding again the reference points.
– Italo Calvino, *Mr Palomar* 1985.

Encouraging an attitude of inquiry and invention in weaving will require, at first, some attention to the work process. There are four distinct stages in creative thinking. We will call them Preparation, Incubation, Visualization and Evaluation. The process is the same whether the scope of the problem being pursued is as broad as developing the premise for a body of work or as minute as choosing the perfect fibre to create the collapse effect for a garment fabric.

For experienced weavers wishing to avoid retreat into pattern books, the production of a truly unique and expressive object will begin with defining personal goals: deciding what the focus of inquiry will be. Product, process or effect (alone or in combination) might be the beginning of the honing of an idea.

The importance of defining the goal cannot be minimized. It can be done intelligently only after a thorough knowledge of cloth structure and a long period of experimentation have given the weaver the necessary background to make creative and legitimate decisions.

During the preparation stage, information is gathered and ideas are assembled. The problem is defined and the known facts relating to the problem are considered critically. In the second stage, incubation, everything is put on hold: ideas may recur, but no action is taken. Visualization involves some form of realization of ideas. This is a difficult stage because sketching or pattern-drafting techniques seldom give enough accurate information, and working directly on the loom is so time-consuming that all possible options can never be tried, leading to the loss of many good ideas. The advent of computer weave programmes and interfaces have solved some of this for pattern weavers: weave structures not tried can be stored in the memory for future use. But for those who haven't become computerized or for whom pattern weaving is not the main goal, there needs to be some consideration of how ideas may be recorded.

The stage of visualization is characterized by divergent thinking: we are interested in generating as many variants on the idea as possible, and in recording these ideas in one or more graphic languages. The weave draft on point paper (see *The Structure of Weaving*) is the language most often used to record and plan weaves. It tells how threads interlace to create the structure of the cloth. However, as every language is a tool, each has its own limitations (like musical scores, the draft cannot speak of texture or colour with any sense of nuance or complexity). Other languages must be used to describe other facets of the work: colour sketches, perhaps swatches of fibre or fabric, points of colour on graph paper, even assemblages of seemingly unrelated materials. Each graphic symbol is always less than what it represents, having a single way of looking at reality. Therefore, understanding the problem is facilitated by using as many different graphic languages as possible.

In another version of the visualization and evaluation stages, Robert McKim (in *Thinking Visually: A Strategy Manual for Problem-Solving*) describes the process as ETC: Express, Test, Cycle. He suggests that no judgements be made during the visualization/sketch stage. After many versions of possible solutions have been expressed, then testing, judging and choosing may occur. Cycling means starting all over again, using convergent thinking, homing in on the best options and expanding upon those.

We've got through the entire creative process without necessarily weaving anything! This may not always be the case: the 'express/illuminate' phase may certainly include sampling on the loom, but this would depend on how finely-tuned the problem has become in the preparation stage. The more specific the limits of the problem, the more specific the visual language of the visualization stage may be. And, of course, experience will eliminate the need for some of the basic information-gathering. In other words, the process is always the same, but it modifies itself according to goals and experiences.

No stage of the process must ever be eliminated, even though it will eventually all become second nature. The very critical stage of testing or revising will later be directed at a finished product, and the cycling will mean producing a number of finished products based on a single premise. Revision of the premise will occur, so that instead of working in a cyclical format, the work pattern becomes a spiral – rather like a glider that has found a thermal updraft, and just as exhilarating.

Various methods of visualizing before weaving used by Geraldine St. Aubyn Hubbard (UK), Diane Sheehan (USA) and Ann Sutton (UK)

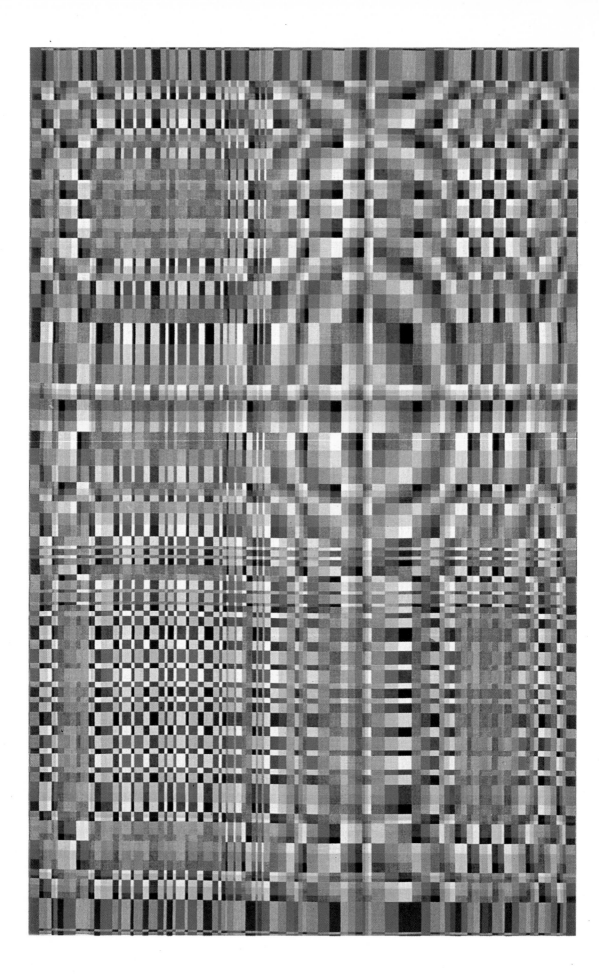

FOCUSING

Weavers usually enjoy working within limitations, and striving to overcome limitations can be the starting point of fine work.

In running a hurdle race, flattening the hurdles is no solution to running a faster race; the purpose has been lost in the solution, and the result is without interest. A solution which incorporates the problem, however, is fascinating to witness.

In weaving, even if the project in mind has no limitations other than those of the loom to be used, setting up some goalposts and defining the size of the field will start to challenge ingenuity and promote solutions. One way to do this is to identify a particular weave, and to examine every permutation possible within its boundaries. Many professional weavers do this for a lifetime, and become fascinated by the exploration of the possibilities within their chosen field. Their fascination invariably passes into the textile. It is interesting to realize how many of the well-known professionals are working in this way, playing every possibility within a very narrow technical field, and being able to generate brilliant ideas within it through sheer familiarity with its capabilities.

Left:
Richard Landis (USA): 'The Sacred and the Profane', 1982. Mercerized sewing thread. 33.5 in × 21.5 in (85 cm × 55 cm). (Photo by Emmit Gowin)
Below:
Richard Landis (USA) (in collaboration with Craig Fuller): 'Nucleus', 1977, 18.5 in × 17 in (47 cm × 43 cm). (Photo by Emmit Gowin. Collection of the Cooper-Hewitt Museum, New York)

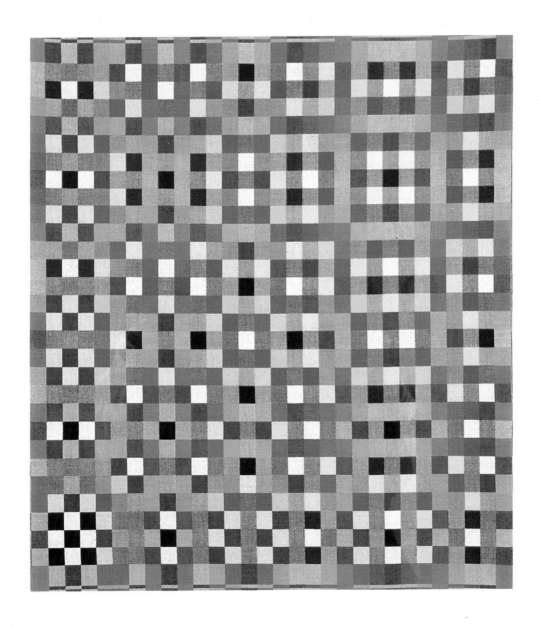

Taking one weave structure, such as double-plain, the possibilities for variation are endless: combinations of yarn, colour, texture, proportion, sett – each contains enough possibilities of exploration for a lifetime's weaving.

1 Mercerized cotton handkerchief, 1987. Kenzo, Japan.
2 Silk and linen curtaining, 'Hologram', 1986. (Jack Lenor Larsen Inc., USA)
3 Cotton, overspun in warp and weft. 'Barkcloth', 1986. (Junichi Arai, Japan)
4 Spun silk, 1984. (Mary Louise Salame, West Surrey College of Art and Design, UK)

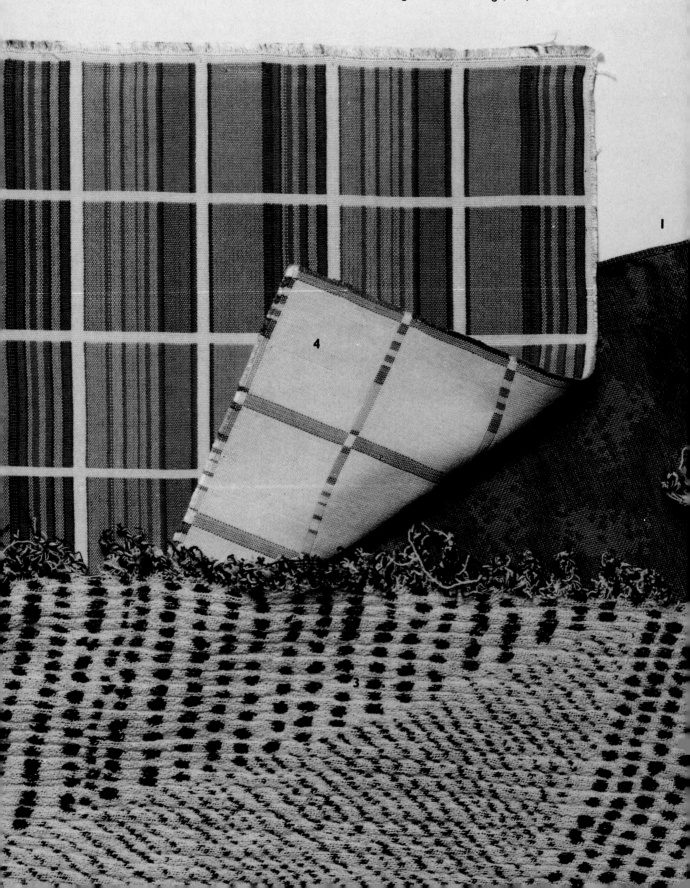

3. INVENTION AND PROCESS

Every stage of the weaving process — from the choice of materials through the finishing of cloth — affords opportunities for creative thinking and invention. What follows is a compendium of ideas and amazing fabrics which are the result of applied genius. The aim is to inspire the reader towards matching this level of critical thinking.

This handwoven scarf in cashmere and silk by Ann Richards (UK) shows an inventive solution to the idea of presenting selvedges, like fins, standing at right angles to the ground cloth. She achieves this by inserting the shuttle several times across the cloth during the placing of each pick. An extra element of interest is in the dyeing of the warp: the ground warp graduates subtly through six colours across the scarf, and the selvedge fins are also dyed in ombré sequence.

THINKING ABOUT MATERIALS

Weavers are familiar with many natural and manmade fibres, and information abounds in every book on textiles It is interesting to consider, however, that almost all plants and most animals bear fibres of some sort, several of which have been used in the past but are no longer regarded as commercially viable. Fragments of information, even legends, can promote new thinking about raw materials and enlarge the ranges of fibres available to the handspinner and weaver.

- Tales of netted *linen* fabrics 'weighing so little that a man's load could cover an entire forest'.
- Remains of very early *hair* yarns show that the fibres were not spun lengthwise, but were placed at right angles to wool fibres, so that they protruded from the base yarn.
- *Silk* is outstanding for certain types of electrical insulation, and large quantities have been used for this purpose.
- The silk of the common *spider* has more tensile strength than steel and has been knitted into very expensive gloves and stockings. Harvesting the fibre from the webs is too labour-intensive to make this fibre commercially viable.
- Piña cloth is made from fibres found in the leaves of the wild *pineapple* plant.
- Fibres can also be obtained from *banana* plants.
- *Human hair* has been used for centuries as a textile fibre, sometimes as a decorative commemoration.
- An early woven fabric found in Greece and Egypt, which has been mistaken for both linen and silk, was found to be made of *byssus,* a glandular secretion of the salt-water mussel. It was woven more recently in Taranata, southern Italy.
- An experimental fibre, Carbofil, was developed in Germany from *horse or ox muscle.*
- Great men, from Alexander to Charlemagne, are said to have enhanced their reputations by the trick of throwing a fine napkin (woven of *asbestos* or *glass*) on to the fire, to remove it later unharmed.

- The invention of manmade fibres was the result of a linking of ideas. In 1884 Count Hilaire de Chardonnet of Paris reasoned that if mulberry leaves (the food of silkworms) were treated with caustic soda (known to make cotton appear silk-like), then artificial silk might be the result. The resulting viscous solution proved his theory. (Later it was realized that the cellulose in the mulberry leaves was also present in other vegetable matter.)
- Early *Chinese silk* fabrics were sold to the Roman Empire, where they were unravelled so that the silk yarn could be used again in more open cloth. (Salome's veils were reputed to have been woven from unravelled silk.)
- A mineral fibre called *Flecton* reflects light at night.
- *Cotton* sewing thread has existed for only about 150 years. James and Patrick Clark, in Paisley, Scotland, were trying to spin a yarn to make smooth, fine and strong heddles for shawl weaving. The result replaced silk sewing thread.
- Cloth is made of very fine shreds of *bamboo* in the Celebes Islands.
- After the First World War, fibres were scarce in Scandinavia, and yarns were made out of *turf.*

Yarns

Alginate Yarns

These yarns have a unique property: they dissolve completely during the finishing process. Made of alginic acid derived from seaweed (and used as a gelling agent in products as diverse as toothpaste and orange squash), it produces a yarn which has many textile uses. It has been used to support wool fibres in fine worsted yarns which were woven in to sheer fabrics; the supporting alginate was then dissolved, leaving an extremely sheer fabric. It is also used in the hosiery trade – a few rows of alginate yarn are knitted in between each sock in continuous production. Washing then separates the socks by dissolving the yarn. Guipure lace is made by embroidering a base cloth made of alginate yarn, which dissolves to leave the embroidery forming a lace cloth.

Handwoven placemat, cotton warp, buntal and knotted raffia weft, 1988. Philippines.

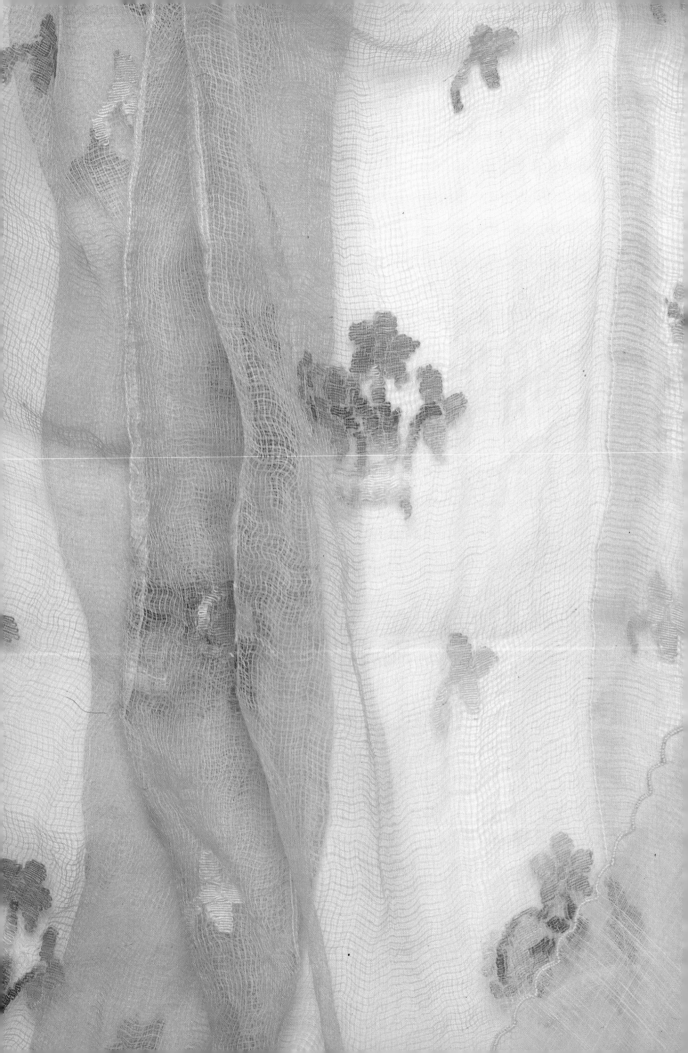

Piña

Almost all plants contain fibres of some sort in their seeds, leaves or stems. Some of these fibres are strong enough to be used as textile fibres, and those which can be easily extracted are used as such. Often the most unlikely plants yield soft fibres: the leaves of the wild pineapple, grown in several parts of the world but predominately in the Philippines, contain strong and lustrous fibres, which are extracted by stripping away the green flesh. The exposed fibres are then scraped clean with a porcelain plate. This fibre is difficult to spin by conventional means, and a yarn is formed by knotting the individual fibres together: a lengthy and time-consuming process. These knotted lengths are then handwoven into fine and strong transparent cloth with a springy character, much prized as one of the rare fabrics of the world.

1 Piña shirt with brocaded silk motifs. Philippines, probably early 20th century.
2 Piña napkin. Philippines.

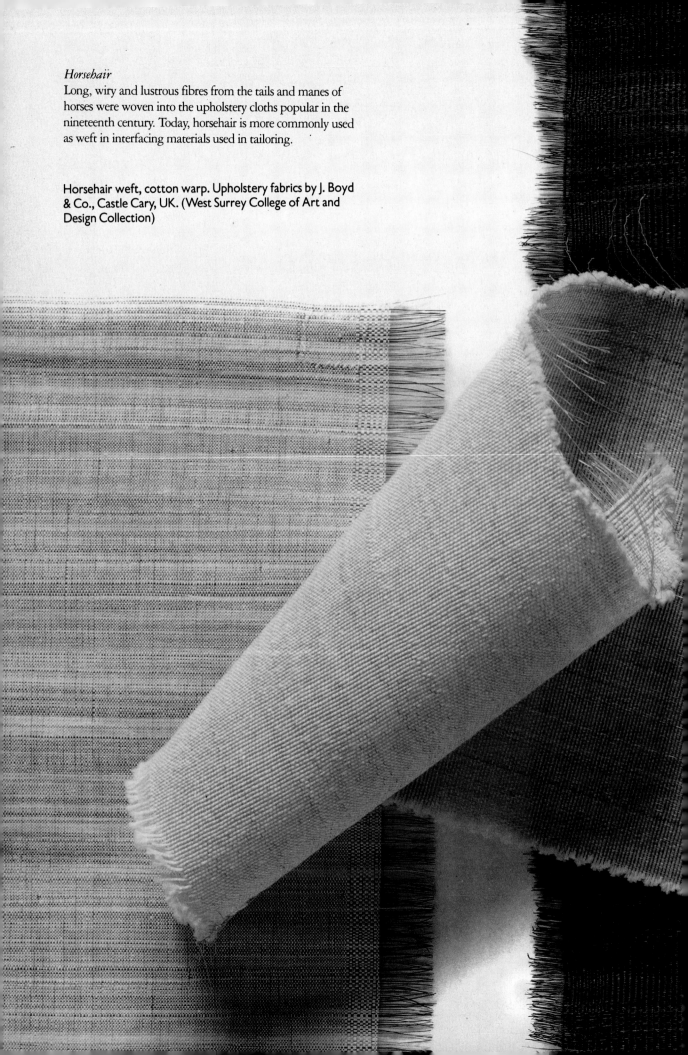

Horsehair

Long, wiry and lustrous fibres from the tails and manes of horses were woven into the upholstery cloths popular in the nineteenth century. Today, horsehair is more commonly used as weft in interfacing materials used in tailoring.

Horsehair weft, cotton warp. Upholstery fabrics by J. Boyd & Co., Castle Cary, UK. (West Surrey College of Art and Design Collection)

Strip Materials

Sheet material such as fabric, leather, polythene, metal film, can all provide weaving materials of any width, by slicing into strips. Even the method of slicing has possibilities.

1,3 Wool yarn and silk/cotton rag warp and weft. (Jilli Blackwood, UK)
2 Handbag fabric: cotton warp, leather strip weft. (Leonarda Capuyan, Philippines)

Paper

Paper can be used in many ways in weaving: strips are twisted and treated with adhesives and water to form a round yarn; sheets are cut finely from edge to edge to form a flat thread. The round yarn was first produced in Saxony in 1895 by Emil Claviez. Called *Xylolin*, it was used extensively in Germany during the First World War for sandbags, cartridge belts and even clothes. Post Second World War, Dora Jung, the Finnish designer, used paper yarns for woven furnishing fabrics. And Japanese paper weaving (*shifu*) is a highly skilled craft, dating from before the Edo period, in which sheets of paper are cut with the grain, nearly from edge to edge. The edges are then broken alternately to give a continuous 'thread', which is sometimes twisted. Japanese weavers use the paper yarn in both warp and weft, and the resulting cloth is soft and washable.

1 Brocade with paper strip weft: monk's stole (*ohi*). Japan, c. 16th century. (Larry Edman Collection)
2 Sample of handmade paper designed for use as weft, in stages of the process. Japan.

2

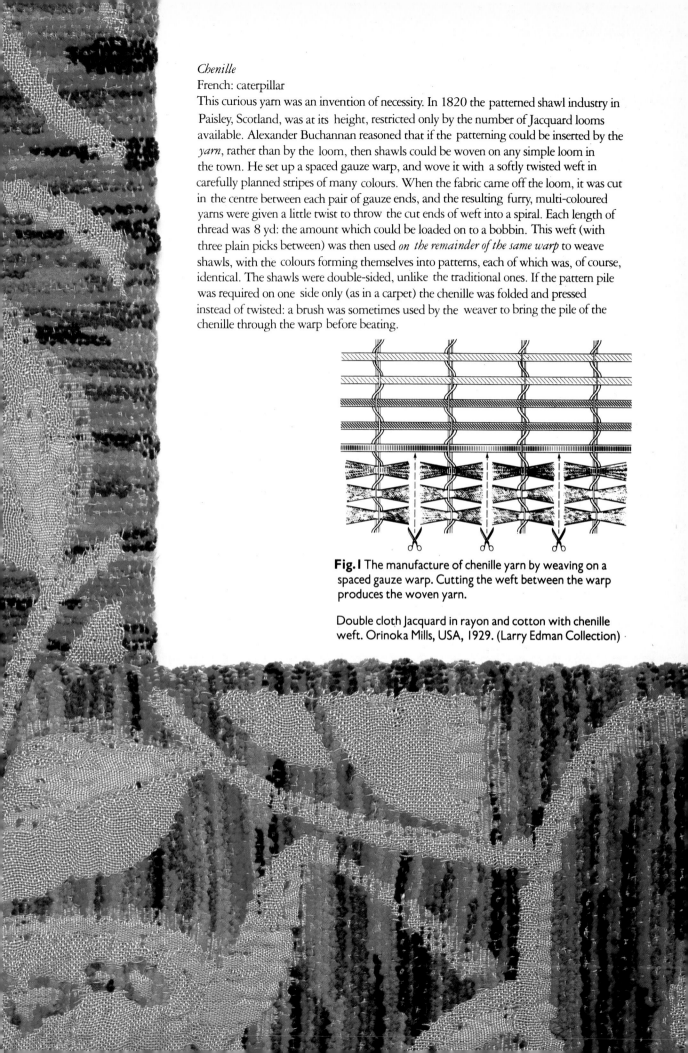

Chenille

French: caterpillar

This curious yarn was an invention of necessity. In 1820 the patterned shawl industry in Paisley, Scotland, was at its height, restricted only by the number of Jacquard looms available. Alexander Buchannan reasoned that if the patterning could be inserted by the *yarn*, rather than by the loom, then shawls could be woven on any simple loom in the town. He set up a spaced gauze warp, and wove it with a softly twisted weft in carefully planned stripes of many colours. When the fabric came off the loom, it was cut in the centre between each pair of gauze ends, and the resulting furry, multi-coloured yarns were given a little twist to throw the cut ends of weft into a spiral. Each length of thread was 8 yd: the amount which could be loaded on to a bobbin. This weft (with three plain picks between) was then used *on the remainder of the same warp* to weave shawls, with the colours forming themselves into patterns, each of which was, of course, identical. The shawls were double-sided, unlike the traditional ones. If the pattern pile was required on one side only (as in a carpet) the chenille was folded and pressed instead of twisted: a brush was sometimes used by the weaver to bring the pile of the chenille through the warp before beating.

Fig.1 The manufacture of chenille yarn by weaving on a spaced gauze warp. Cutting the weft between the warp produces the woven yarn.

Double cloth Jacquard in rayon and cotton with chenille weft. Orinoka Mills, USA, 1929. (Larry Edman Collection)

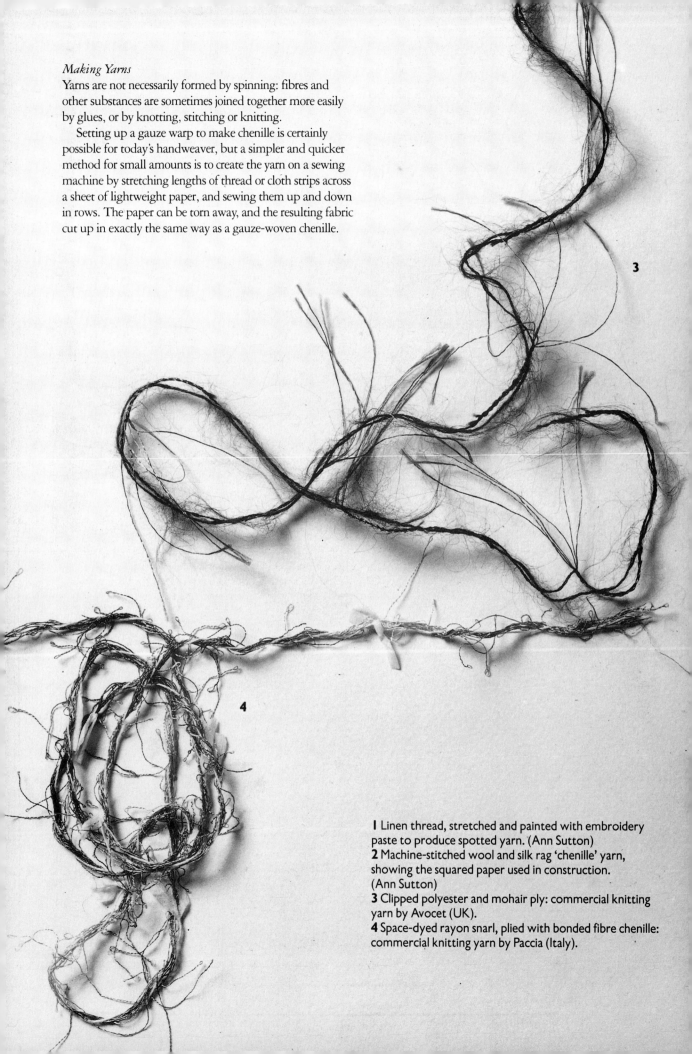

Making Yarns

Yarns are not necessarily formed by spinning: fibres and other substances are sometimes joined together more easily by glues, or by knotting, stitching or knitting.

Setting up a gauze warp to make chenille is certainly possible for today's handweaver, but a simpler and quicker method for small amounts is to create the yarn on a sewing machine by stretching lengths of thread or cloth strips across a sheet of lightweight paper, and sewing them up and down in rows. The paper can be torn away, and the resulting fabric cut up in exactly the same way as a gauze-woven chenille.

1 Linen thread, stretched and painted with embroidery paste to produce spotted yarn. (Ann Sutton)
2 Machine-stitched wool and silk rag 'chenille' yarn, showing the squared paper used in construction. (Ann Sutton)
3 Clipped polyester and mohair ply: commercial knitting yarn by Avocet (UK).
4 Space-dyed rayon snarl, plied with bonded fibre chenille: commercial knitting yarn by Paccia (Italy).

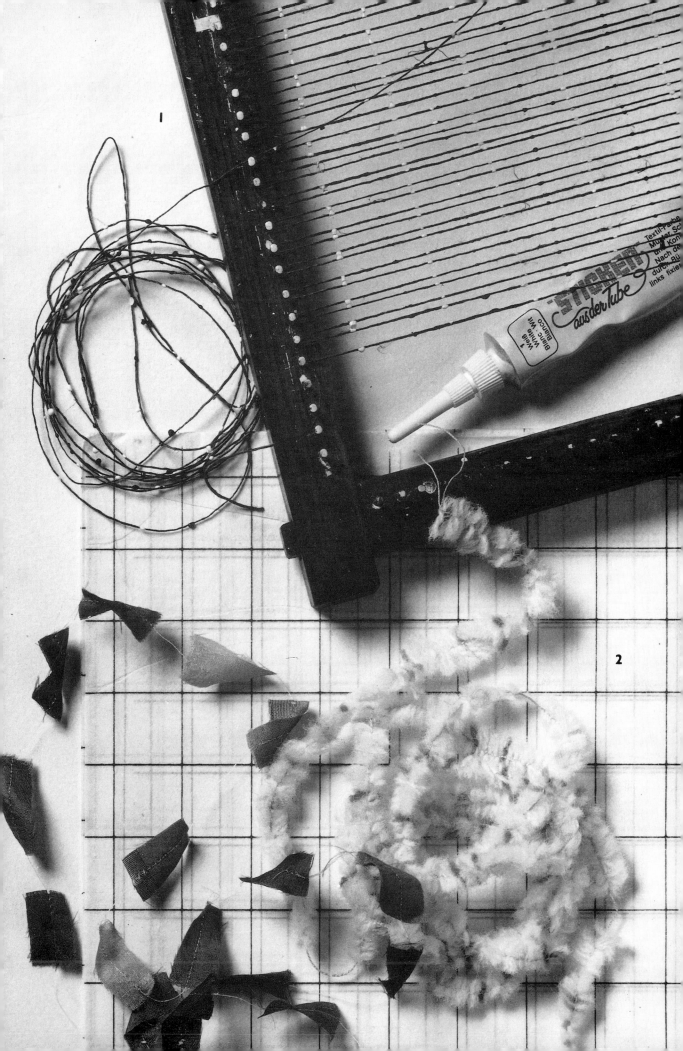

1 Quadruple weave cotton scarf with overspun weft.
(Junichi Arai, Japan)

2 S and Z overspun merino wool warp with silk bands,
overspun merino weft. (Erica Hartman, West Surrey
College of Art and Design, UK)
3 Warp-spaced twill, silk warp and overspun cotton singles
weft. (Marilyn Pettit, West Surrey College of Art and
Design, UK)

Overspun Yarns
During the spinning of a yarn, twist is given to the fibres in
order to hold them together and to give strength. Putting in
more twist than is necessary for this purpose results in harder
yarns, but can also lead to an excess of energy, usually
revealed by the tendency of the relaxed yarn to kink and coil
in an attempt to twist with itself and so release the tensions
built up during the spinning. Handspinners are more
familiar with this, as most commercial weaving yarns have
been set by heat under tension to make them docile in use.
(The difference in twist applied to commercial yarns
destined for knitting and for weaving is soon discovered by
the beginner: 'hosiery twist' when woven produces a flat
cloth with a 'soapy' appearance; 'weave twist' when closely
knitted can result in shapes which are diagonally distorted.)

●八丁撚糸機

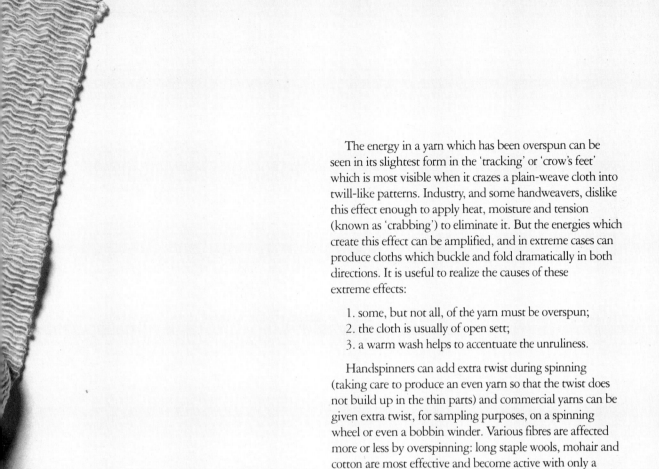

The energy in a yarn which has been overspun can be seen in its slightest form in the 'tracking' or 'crow's feet' which is most visible when it crazes a plain-weave cloth into twill-like patterns. Industry, and some handweavers, dislike this effect enough to apply heat, moisture and tension (known as 'crabbing') to eliminate it. But the energies which create this effect can be amplified, and in extreme cases can produce cloths which buckle and fold dramatically in both directions. It is useful to realize the causes of these extreme effects:

1. some, but not all, of the yarn must be overspun;
2. the cloth is usually of open sett;
3. a warm wash helps to accentuate the unruliness.

Handspinners can add extra twist during spinning (taking care to produce an even yarn so that the twist does not build up in the thin parts) and commercial yarns can be given extra twist, for sampling purposes, on a spinning wheel or even a bobbin winder. Various fibres are affected more or less by overspinning: long staple wools, mohair and cotton are most effective and become active with only a small amount of overtwist; care must be taken with silk to ensure that the dynamism doesn't release itself into a corkscrew; manmade fibres are the least effective. In all cases, a single yarn is more dynamic than a plied one.

Overspun yarns are not the easiest to weave. Used as warp they are extremely unmanageable unless kept permanently under tension during beaming and entering. The twist energy will run out of a cut end with alacrity. Sizing can be of great help in controlling twist activity until the size is dissolved in the finishing wash. Cotton, for example, can be starched.

Sash (*obi*) fabric of silk with overspun weft. Japan.
Inset: Equipment used to add extra twist to yarns. Japan.

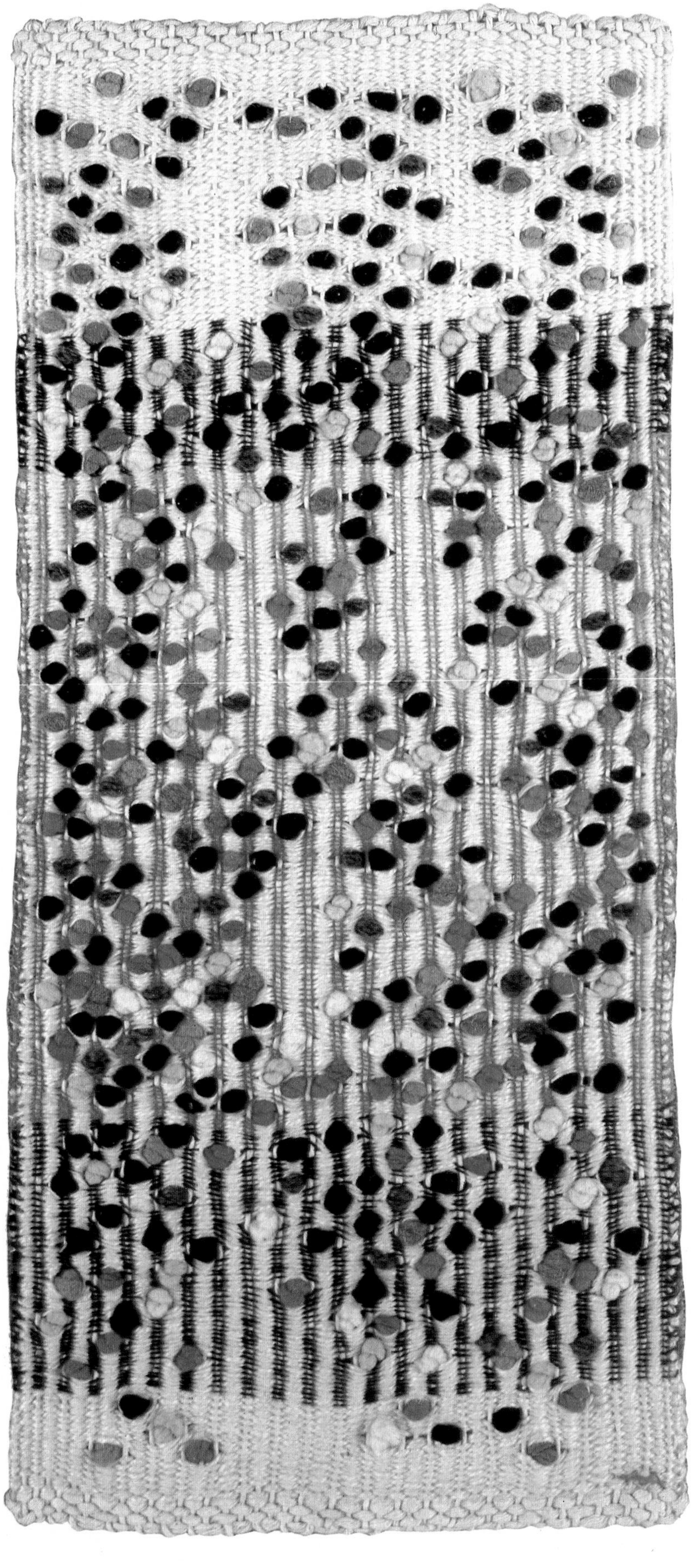

Investigation and Experiment

Fibre artists can act as researchers using outrageous combinations of materials and time-consuming processes that traditional fabric weavers never consider. All investigations and inventions can be springboards for expanded uses. For instance, Anni Albers' work at the Bauhaus was concerned with new materials and changing the character of familiar materials. Ed Rossbach is known for his use of the products of contemporary culture, daring to weave with discarded remnants of consumer life.

Often there is no real reason, other than tradition, for certain threads to be used in the weft only. Ingenuity may be needed to make use of the material in the warp, but the results will certainly be worthwhile. For example, early elastic tape was made for many years with rubber in the weft, so that the stretch was across the tape only. By putting the rubber threads in the warp, a much more useful product was achieved, and a whole industry founded.

Above right:
Ed Rossbach: 'Homage to Dorothy Leibes', c.1969, polyethylene tubes stuffed with various food containers, twines, etc . . . (Photo by the artist. Collection of the artist)

Right: Detail

Left:
Anni Albers: Pictorial weaving 'Dotted', 1959, repp-woven ground with multicoloured knots. 23.75 in × 11 in (60 cm × 28 cm). (Collection of Mr and Mrs Ralph W. Bettelheim, New York)

These study samples by Lena Bergstrom (Konstfackskolan, Stockholm) explore the combinations of such diverse materials as rubber strip and tube, cotton, wool, polypropylene, sisal etc., as well as the different sett ratios which these combinations necessitate. Constant and simple colouring is maintained throughout, and the double-cloth structure is used in all the examples, leaving the variety within the study to be provided by the materials alone.

Colour

Woven colour is unique and complex. Unlike applying paint to a uniform surface such as stretched canvas or paper, colour in weaving is carried by yarns which can vary considerably in surface, size and shape. An organic connection exists between the colour and the surface, because while the design is being constructed so is the pliable plane in which it exists.

As there is no technical reason why each warp and weft in a handwoven cloth cannot be of a different colour, minute particles of many colours may be juxtaposed. Add to this variations made possible by changes in weave structure, using multiple layers of weaving or supplementary warps and wefts. Each structural change carries the potential for colour change.

Our response to colour can be explained both objectively and subjectively. Colour theory books abound, but the best colour schemes often defy analysis. Although there is no substitute for experience and practice, a few basic principles deserve mention since they are especially relevant for the weaver.

Silk scarf with printed warp. (Fiona Wormal, West Surrey College of Art and Design, UK)

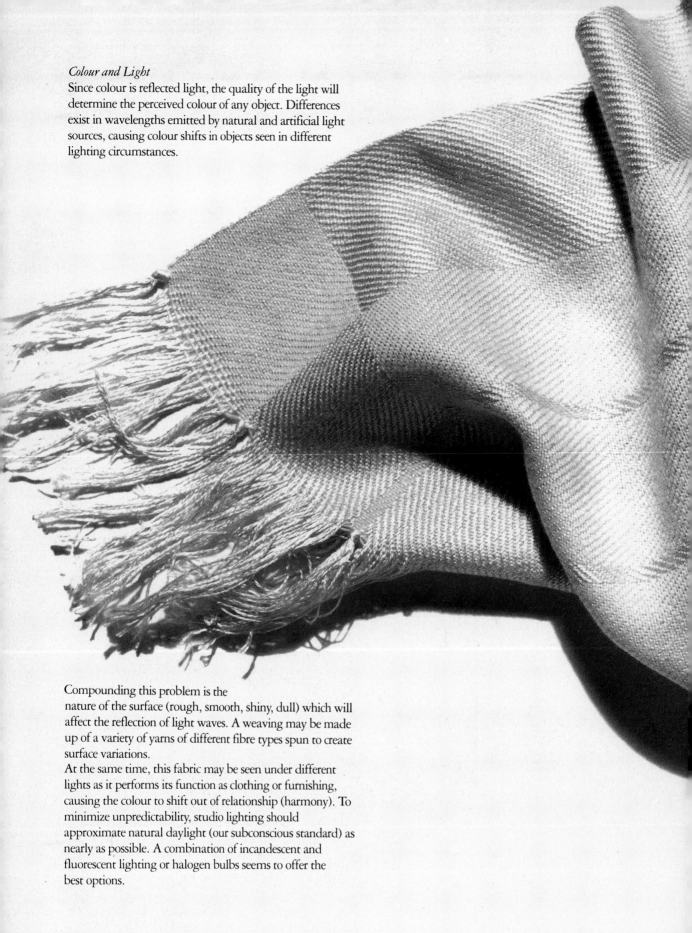

Colour and Light
Since colour is reflected light, the quality of the light will determine the perceived colour of any object. Differences exist in wavelengths emitted by natural and artificial light sources, causing colour shifts in objects seen in different lighting circumstances.

Compounding this problem is the
nature of the surface (rough, smooth, shiny, dull) which will affect the reflection of light waves. A weaving may be made up of a variety of yarns of different fibre types spun to create surface variations.
At the same time, this fabric may be seen under different lights as it performs its function as clothing or furnishing, causing the colour to shift out of relationship (harmony). To minimize unpredictability, studio lighting should approximate natural daylight (our subconscious standard) as nearly as possible. A combination of incandescent and fluorescent lighting or halogen bulbs seems to offer the best options.

Silk and wool twill scarf. (Geraldine St. Aubyn Hubbard, UK)

Colour Quantity

The amount of colour in relationship to surrounding colours can greatly affect the perceived hue. Different quantities of colour will change the way those colours are perceived.

   Colours in woven cloth often appear in pixels: tiny dots of juxtaposed colour which tend to blend visually to create mixtures. This phenomenon is known as *optical blending*, and controlling it can be a great challenge for the weaver.

1 Three cloths which use the same colours in different quantities and positions. (Julie Langham, West Surrey College of Art and Design, UK)
2 Cotton Jacquard portrait in which colour-mixing is controlled by a computer process developed by Karl Noonan. (Sophis Design Systems, Belgium)

1

Tone/Value

The choice of colour (the hue) often has much less to do with its impact on a colour scheme than with the relative lightness or darkness of that hue. This is true because of the effect of extremely light or extremely dark tones (values) on adjacent colours (see Simultaneous Contrast) and because so much of our perception of depth in the world depends on light and shade.

A value-finder (grey scale) is very useful to the weaver; it enables accurate and quantifiable judgements to be made about the comparative values of any yarns.

The Grey Scale An ordinary office punch can be used to make two holes in each of the bands on a scale, such as the one shown opposite. To judge the value of a yarn or fabric, place the scale over the cone or skein pressing tightly so that there is little shadow or gradation of light on the surface below. Squinting will cut out most of the light reaching the eye so that colour perception will be minimized. Note the number of the band in which the edge of the hole (the line between the grey and the surface below) is the least distinct. This may take some practice at first, but careful comparison and a process of elimination will soon make the best match apparent. To find another colour of the same value, repeat the process.

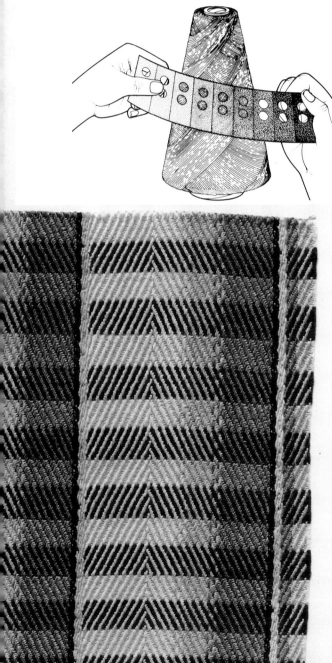

I

1 Silk, wool and linen fabric, with values organized to create a three-dimensional illusion. (Lesley Burtenshaw, West Surrey College of Art and Design, UK)
2 Plain weave shirting, using two colours in elaborate sequence to provide a tonal range.

2

Simultaneous Contrast

Colour exists in context and the context affects the colour. This basic rule was first established by Michel Eugene Chevreul who, in his capacity as Superintendent of Dyeing at the Royal Tapestry Manufactories (Gobelins) of France, sought a reason for the apparent loss of depth and richness in black yarns produced in his workshop after they had been woven into the fabric. The answer lay in the colours used in conjunction with these yarns, which, because they were rich blues and purples, caused the blacks to take on a brownish cast. He published the results of his investigations into colour perception in *The Laws of Contrast of Colour* in 1839. In very brief summary, adjoining colours were found to affect each other in hue, brightness and tone, maximizing the inherent difference between the colours. Dark and light tones placed next to each other will cause the dark to appear darker and the light to appear lighter. Intense hues will force contiguous hues to take on the complement (hence the warm brown tone taken on by Chevreul's black when placed next to cool blues and purples).

1 Silk twill, in which the constant pink supplementary warp appears to change colour as it is affected by the adjacent warp and weft crossings. (Bridget Worthington, West Surrey College of Art and Design, UK)
2 Two samples showing the effect that light and dark value changes have on the adjacent colours. (Eva Pettigrew, West Surrey College of Art and Design, UK)

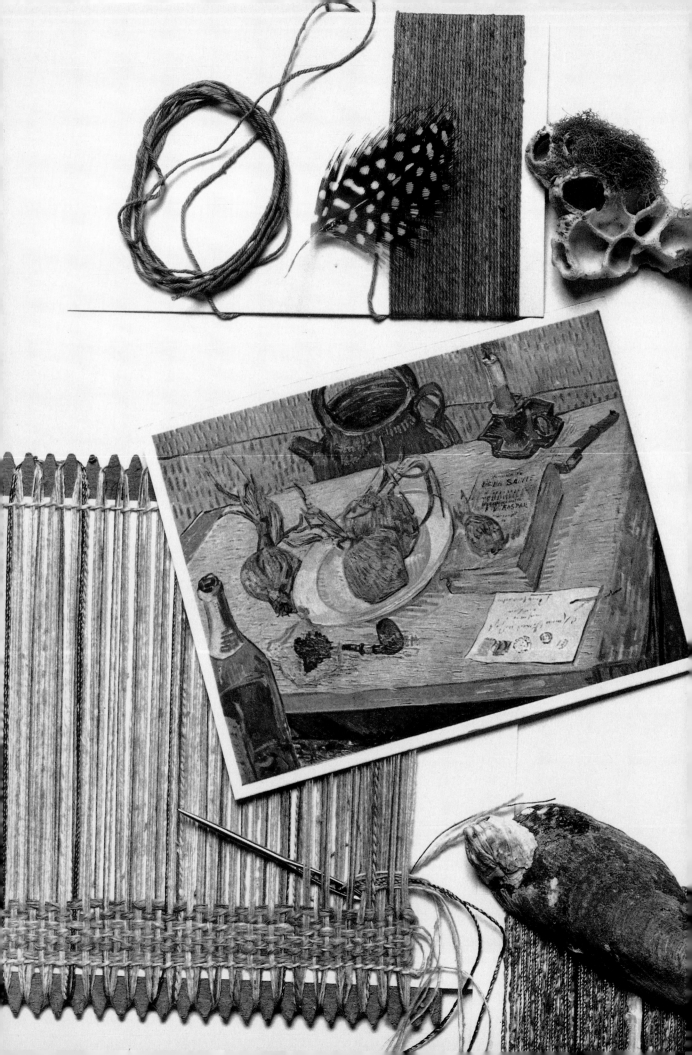

Colour Studies

These colour studies, designed especially for the weaver, are elaborations upon Elsa Regensteiner's 'warp sequences'. However, the goal here is not to design a warp, but to develop an eye for subtle colour differences and an ability to balance colour quantities. The approach here should be to study intensely each nuance of colour, avoiding the natural tendency to generalize and simplify rather than actually seeing what is there. Setting down the results of these investigations in the materials of weaving (yarns) rather than paint removes any distracting problems of handling an unfamiliar medium, and enables consideration of texture, scale and sheen as well as colour.

Natural objects have been chosen for the first study because nature provides an endless source of practically fool-proof colour schemes. It is recommended that these objects be inanimate, rocks and shells for instance rather than flowers which may change colour over the time a detailed study can take. See page 82 for complete instructions.

The finished study should resemble as closely as possible the colour and surface quality of the object. To do this it may be necessary to modify the yarns: plying to blend colour or unplying to provide a thinner yarn. Surfaces may be changed by abrading the yarn or even by tying knots in it to increase the texture. Colours should be evenly distributed over the base ground, even if they are fairly isolated in the object, so that the eye has to judge and balance colours. Placing individual threads across the surface instead of the more usual method of winding ensures a more sensitive balance of colour and position.

It will be noticed that colours work to alter each other when juxtaposed. The position of a single thread in relationship to surrounding colours can be critical to the hue that is perceived. An ability to recognize and control optical blending and simultaneous contrast will be developed through these studies.

Another version of colour investigation can be undertaken using postcard reproductions of paintings by master artists. These are more challenging because the range of hues is usually broader, and the colour balancing more critical. A postcard version of the image is preferable to a larger reproduction as it presents colours in quantities which are more easily accessible for translation in this study.

To relate these studies more directly to what happens when colour blends in woven cloth, small needle weavings may be constructed on simple nail or card looms. These cloths become woven abstractions of nature or paintings and can lead to surprisingly original uses of colour and texture. See page 83 for complete instructions.

1 Ruth J. Winsor; Newfoundland
2 Barbara Roberts; Newfoundland
3 Nadine Mills; Newfoundland
4 Lillian Whelan; Newfoundland
  (Painting: Hugo Van Der Goes. Adoration of the
  Shepherds: detail. Uffizi Gallery, Florence)

5 Ruth J. Winsor; Newfoundland
  (Painting: Balthus: Artist and his model: Musee National
  d'Art Moderne, Centre Georges Pompidou, Paris)
6 Andy St. John; Newfoundland
  (Painting: Kees van Dangen: Madjesko, Soprano singer
  1908: Museum of Modern Art, New York)

1

2

3

4

5

6

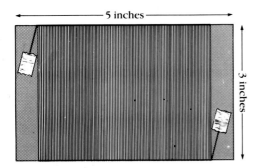

Fig.1

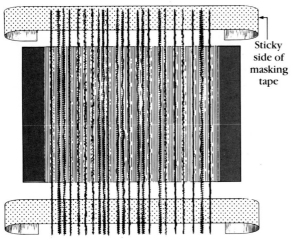

Sticky side of masking tape

Fig.2

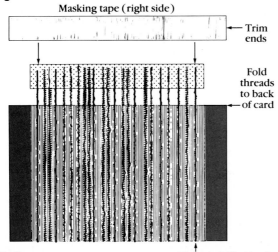

Masking tape (right side)

← Trim ends

Fold threads to back of card

Threads folded back

Fig.3

Colour Study Diagrams

Fig.1 A piece of mounting card (mat board) measuring approximately 3 in × 5 in (8 cm × 13 cm) is used as a basis for the study. Work over an area which leaves a short space at each end of the card. After examining the object on a plain and neutral ground (this is critical to eliminate any interference which even simple pattern or pale colour could provide), a yarn of simple structure is chosen which matches the overall colour and tone (value) of the object. This yarn is wrapped closely from near one end to the other to provide a base coat over which the colour field of yarn can be developed.

Fig.2 Pieces of masking tape 11 in (28 cm) long are folded into loops, sticky side out, and placed above and below the wrapped card, which rests face up on the same neutral ground as the object. Individual threads are then chosen to match the colour, texture scale and sheen found in the object, and placed on the tapes so that they extend across the face of the card.

Fig.3 When these tapes are full, or the study complete, the yarns may be fastened to the card by trimming them close to the tapes, placing a new piece of masking tape across the ends of the threads and cutting the tape loops at the folds. The threads can then be folded around the back of the card and adhered there.

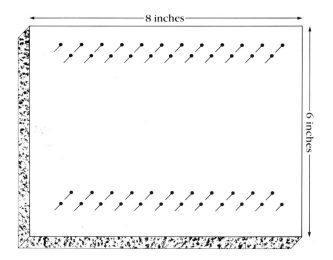

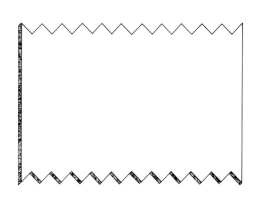

Fig.1

Woven Colour Study Diagrams

Fig.1 Using a small rectangle of chipboard (pressed wood particle board) as a base, drive in a 6-in (15-cm) long row of nails (use 3/4-in (2-cm) long brads or nails with very small heads. Let them stand about 1/4 in (0.6 cm) from the surface of the board. Another parallel row should be driven 5 in (13 cm) down the board. (Alternatively, use a simple serrated card loom.)

Fig.2 Choose warp threads for their relationship to the object or painting studied, and grouping them in twos and threes so that the warp is a blend, begin to wind them around the nails as shown. The number of threads used will depend on the spacing of the nails and the thickness of the threads, but the result should provide a yarn which is the same size as the space between the yarns to give a sett for a balanced weave (see pages 8-11: *The Structure of Weaving* by Ann Sutton)

It is helpful to insert a row or two of twining in order to set the warp spacing before weaving begins. It will also help to strengthen the cloth edge when it is removed from the loom.

Fig.3 Darning needles, bodkins, or tapestry needles with blunt tips may be used to weave in the weft, which should also consist of multiple yarns. The aim is to produce a balanced cloth in which the colour and texture match closely the object or painting being studied. When complete, the fabric can be removed from the loom by prying the warps off with the tip of the needle.

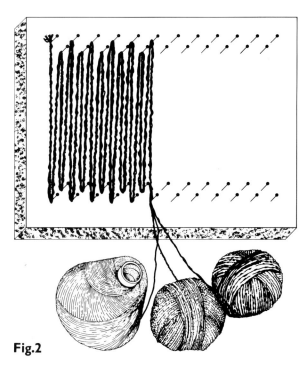

Fig.2

Fig.3

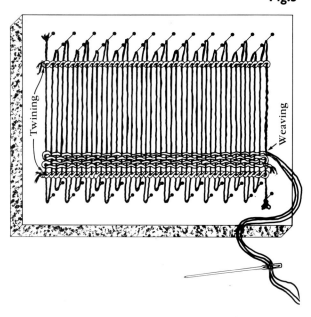

Special Colouring Processes

Colour is an important element in any woven textile, and it is usually provided by the process of dyeing at any stage in the manufacture, from fibres through to finished cloth.

One way to produce a coloured yarn is to dye the fibres before spinning, but sometimes fibres produce the colour naturally: cotton, for instance, is usually white or pale brown in its natural colour. However, in about 1550, Don Pedro Gutiérrez de Santa Clara reported from Spain: 'There is in this country much cotton which of itself is blue, brown, tawny, yellow, and the colour is so fine that it is something to be noted, as though it had been in dye for a long time for the painter of the world gave to it those vivid colours.'

Sometimes nature can be helped: it was discovered in the nineteenth century that if the food given to silkworms was itself dyed, the colour of the silk was affected. By dyeing the mulberry leaves with madder, the cocoon became yellow; indigo produced a greenish-yellow silk; madder plus indigo made the silk bright green; and cochineal-dyed mulberry leaves produced an orange fibre. This must have been the idea (in itself revolutionary) which later supported the idea of dope-dyeing manmade fibres.

Dye can be applied to:

1. The fibres before spinning (known as stock-dyeing). This stage allows the possibility of mixing several coloured fibres together to blend a colour within the yarn: this is arguably the liveliest colour of all. In industry, the fibres are often arranged as 'tops', loose ropes of fibre, wound on perforated spindles and placed in a tank where dye is pumped backwards and forwards through the fibres. Manmade fibres are often 'solution-dyed' or 'dope-dyed': pigment is introduced to the spinning solution before extrusion.

2. The yarn before weaving. This will give perfectly even coloured yarns which can produce a cloth which is 'colour woven'. Industrially, the yarns can be dyed in the conventional hank form, but can also be wound up to 2 lb (1 kilo), on perforated cones or tubes, and dyed under pressure. Some warp yarns are dyed on large perforated drums.

3. The cloth during finishing. This 'piece-dyeing' provides the possibility for cross-dyed effects, where the cloth, having been woven in fibres which react to different types of dyes, can be dyed in multi-colours, *in one dyebath*, by the affinity of different fibres to the various coloured dyes which have been mixed together.

It is interesting to consider the possibilities of colouring textiles by substances other than dye: a starting point might be to consider the virtually ineradicable stains and marks which can be acquired by accident such as paint or blood.

Some fibres are difficult to dye, and ingenious solutions have been found to overcome their resistance. Linen cloth is sometimes soaked with dye and run through a bath of molten metal so that the weight will ensure thorough impregnation of the fibres by the dye.

Contrary to popular thinking, dye need not be 'fast'. The dye in denim jeans is 'guaranteed to fade', and the dyes in true Madras cottons are advertised as 'bleeding'.

Resist dyeing is a favourite trick of the handweaver, and this, too, can be applied at all stages of production.

1. In fibre form: 'rainbow dyeing' is already popular – it was discovered that locks of wool fleece in grease could be stacked, points down, in a pan, and sprinkled with different coloured dyestuffs before being heated. Enterprising weavers have also discovered the potential of the microwave oven in this context.

2. In yarn form: conventionally, parts of the warp or hank are bound with impervious material (raffia, polythene, rubber, tightly-wound string) so that the dye cannot penetrate them. In 1845, Louis Schwabe, in Manchester, was printing skeins of yarn to produce random speckling and mottling in the woven fabric. Yarn can be knitted quickly, printed and then unravelled to produce dyed areas. Warps can be made and printed before being woven; this process has been a favourite of industry where the unwoven warp can be run in sheet form through the printing rollers. Handweavers may find it more convenient to weave the warp very loosely before printing it on a table or even tie-dyeing it. This weft can then be removed as the warp is replaced on the loom.

In the early nineteenth century, Richard Whytock of Edinburgh replaced the extravagant five colours which ran along the back of Wilton carpets with a single yarn which he printed in carefully-judged stripes on the warp yarns wound round a huge drum. When woven into pile, the coloured areas of warp formed into patterns as planned.

It is valuable to think of all the different ways in which a yarn could be dyed in some areas, with other areas left undyed. Clamps have been used for this purpose, and still are in Japan for 'kasuri'. An old Japanese technique is to weave a close cloth with a cotton warp and silk weft, dye it, and then bury it in the ground. The cotton rots, leaving the silk as a mottled yarn which can be woven up into another cloth.

3. In fabric form: when the fabric has been woven it can be printed, tie-dyed, or in other ways treated in areas with dye, while other areas remain undyed.

Cotton kimono fabric: the ikat-dyed weft is planned to give areas of four different values, using only one colour in the dyeing. Japan.

Combining Techniques

The linking of two common techniques in weaving can often lead to one good new one. Combining a yarn-colouring technique with a structural technique has, both in the past and today, created fabrics of integrity and magic. One particular combination, that of 'warp painting' and 'velvet pile', has been taken to extraordinary lengths. In order to understand the achievements of Gaspard Grégoire, it is necessary to examine a simpler example: the small Japanese velvet purse. In this the design blocks measure about one-inch in the direction of the warp. As will be realized from the section on velvet-weaving on page 110, the warp forming the velvet pile must be about seven times the length of the ground warp. In the Japanese velvet, therefore, the warp would be bound, or otherwise resisted from accepting the dye, in areas which would be one-inch wide but seven-inches long. When woven into velvet, this would produce a one-inch square block. (In the example, the block was also 'pulled' to produce the characteristic diagonally-stepped motif, the centre of which has been pulled so that the colours reverse their positions.)

2

1 Gaspard Gregoire: Madonna and Child (from a painting). Painted warp woven in velvet technique miniaturizes the image. France, early 19th century. (Victoria and Albert Museum, London: T260-1960)
2 Purse in ikat velvet. Japan, 19th century.

42 inches

42 inches

42 inches

8½ inches

8½ inches

In the early nineteenth century, a Frenchman, Gaspard Grégoire, weaving in Aix-en-Provence, took a similar combination of techniques and achieved remarkable results. He would copy a painting of the time (a portrait of Napoleon, or of Louis XVIII, or a classical figure) on to the velvet warp before weaving. A classical figure, for instance, would be lifesize: 5 ft 6 in to 5 ft 9 in tall. To weave this warp into velvet would result in an inelegant, very squat figure, so before weaving Grégoire would select every fifth thread, and enter these ends in the loom in sequence, so that, when woven, this elongated image would become a perfectly proportioned figure in velvet about 10. in tall. The remaining threads would then be similarly selected, and woven, and an 'edition' of five, seemingly identical, images could be produced in this way from one painted warp.

This is an assumption of the technique used; exact details are unknown since the artist destroyed his papers and 'secrets' before he died. Examples can be found in the Victoria and Albert Museum, London; the Metropolitan Museum of Art, New York; the Cooper-Hewitt Museum, New York; and the Minneapolis Institute of Art.

Fig.1 Gregoire miniaturises the image by taking every fifth end of the painted warp and foreshortens the resulting elongated image by weaving in as velvet.

Fig.2 Warp preparation for velvet purse (see p.89).

Fig.1

90

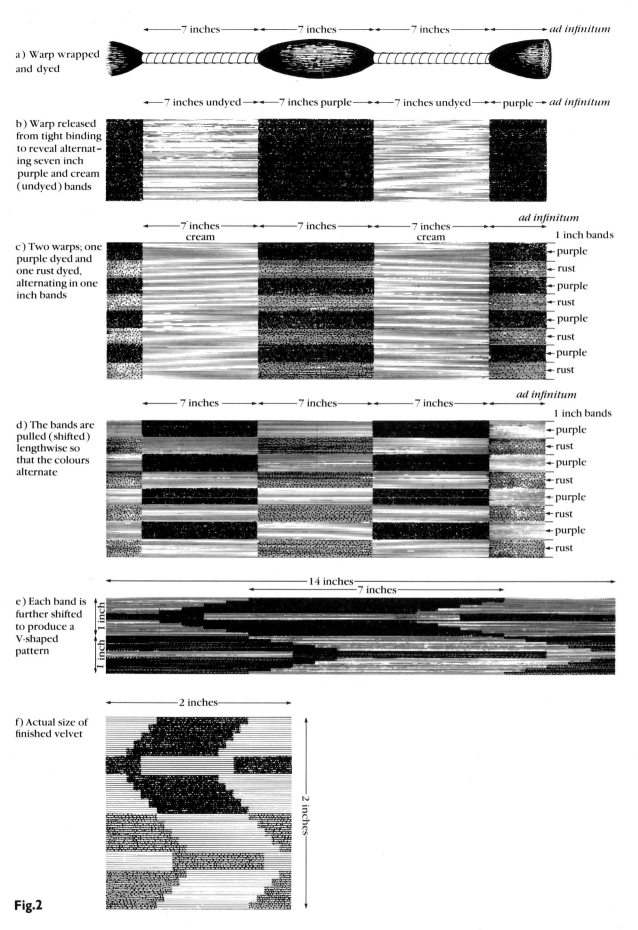

a) Warp wrapped and dyed

← 7 inches → ← 7 inches → ← 7 inches → ← *ad infinitum*

← 7 inches undyed → ← 7 inches purple → ← 7 inches undyed → ← purple → *ad infinitum*

b) Warp released from tight binding to reveal alternating seven inch purple and cream (undyed) bands

← 7 inches cream → ← 7 inches → ← 7 inches cream → *ad infinitum*

1 inch bands
← purple
← rust
← purple
← rust
← purple
← rust
← purple
← rust

c) Two warps; one purple dyed and one rust dyed, alternating in one inch bands

← 7 inches → ← 7 inches → ← 7 inches → *ad infinitum*

1 inch bands
← purple
← rust
← purple
← rust
← purple
← rust
← purple
← rust

d) The bands are pulled (shifted) lengthwise so that the colours alternate

← 14 inches →
← 7 inches →

e) Each band is further shifted to produce a V-shaped pattern

1 inch
1 inch
1 inch

← 2 inches →

f) Actual size of finished velvet

2 inches

Fig.2

91

TOOL MODIFICATION

Throughout history, some of the most interesting textiles have been made with unconventional equipment: looms and smaller textile tools can be altered to suit the weaver's needs. Sometimes the alteration is small, at other times considerable. The makers of looms produce looms for the majority; it is up to individual weavers to question each part on the loom in their search for a personal approach to weaving. Every item, with the possible exception of the side frames, can be altered or removed to dramatic effect.

1 Curtaining fabric in spaced ondulé warp bands, in plain and twill weaves held in place by pairs of leno ends. Synthetic fibre. Commercially woven, probably in USA. (Larry Edman Collection)
2 Ondulé dress fabric. Japan, 20th century. (Ken Colwell Collection)

2

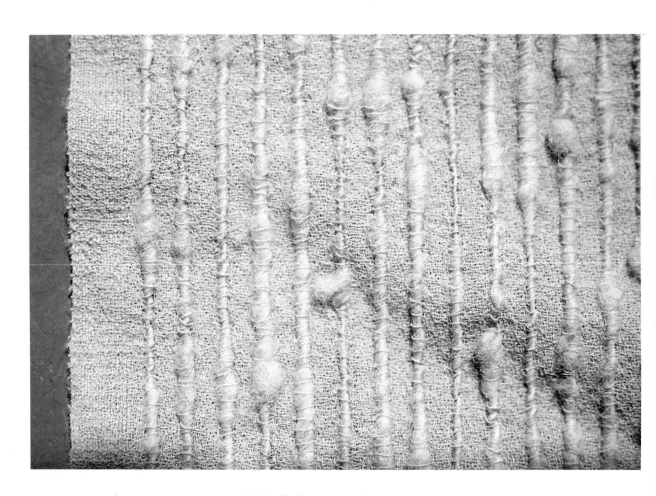

I Woollen dress fabric, handwoven in the 1930s by Rodier
(France), showing the use of thick and irregular handspun
yarns in the warp, alongside fine crêpe spun threads. This
fabric was probably woven with the aid of a special reed.

The Loom

The loom is not a single invention but the result of a long series of improvements. — A. C. Weibel, *Two Thousand Years of Textiles*, 1952.

The primary functions of the loom are:

1. to hold the warp *in place* and under *tension*;
2. to allow certain threads to be raised forming a *shed* for the passage of the shuttle; and
3. to provide a mechanism for beating or laying the weft in place.

Most of the refinements to the loom have been in the elaboration of the shedding process which allows for ever more complicated structures to be woven. We will concentrate on the other two critical loom functions which weavers have some ability to control and modify for themselves whether their looms be 2-shaft counterbalance or 36-shaft dobbies.

The Reed

A device consisting of a number of wires closely set between two slats or baulks, which may serve any or all of the following purposes: separating the warp threads; determining the spacing of the warp threads; guiding the shuttle; and beating up the weft. — The Textile Institute, *Textile Terms and Definitions, 1963.*

Background

In early reeds, dents were made of reed or cane, split by pressing them against a taper spindle which had knives radiating from it set at appropriate distances. In 1733, John Kay substituted flat brass or iron wire, and the resulting stronger reed enabled accurate weaving of finer cloth.

The wires are set, usually vertically, between pairs of half-round wooden rods at top and bottom. They are bound in place with tarred or waxed cord passing between the wires and around the rods. The thickness of the cord determines the spacing between the dents. The completed top and bottom baulks are then usually coated with pitch or resin to stabilize the construction, before being covered with paper.

Developments took place in the dent wires. It was realized that they ought not to be perfectly round in section, or like a flat strip, but thicker in the middle and tapering to either edge, like a leaf. This diminished the friction on the warp threads and also eased the passage of any irregularity or small knot in the warp yarn.

Reeds were sometimes made double, with two sets of wires spaced by laths, so that those of one set faced the spaces of the other, in an attempt 'to prevent loose fibres from matting together and choking the threads'.

In 1845, Clinton Gilroy was advocating 'loose' reeds for weaving lightweight fabrics:

In weaving light fabrics of cloth the upper rib of the reed is not confined in the shell of the lay, but a light shaft of wood with a groove is used. To each end of this shaft is fixed, at right angles, a thin flat piece of wood, which springs easily backward and forward. The extremities of these pieces are nailed to the back of the swords of the lay, and a cord is tied round both, by which the degree of spring may be regulated, the rib of the reed is received into this groove, and the shell is to be used above the vibrating reed, serving merely as a rest for the weaver's left hand to work the lay. Thus the reed yields and stops the cloth being too thick. On even lighter cloth, a woollen cord is stretched between the two swords, and the top of the reed is tied to that. — Clinton Gilroy, *The Art of Weaving (by Hand and by Power)*, 1845.

It is possible to modify the reed in many different ways, each one of which will give dramatic results in a woven cloth, even when used with a plain weave structure. Combinations of these modifications are also possible.

Unwilling to allow any part of his machine to pass without contributing something to the realisation of his artistic desires, the weaver has made the reed serve him in several ways. — William S. Murphy, *The Textile Industries*, vol. 5, 1911.

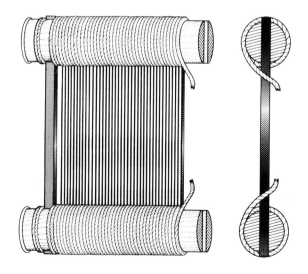

Fig. I Traditional construction of a reed. The wooden baulks were subsequently covered with pitch and a protective paper.

Reed Modification

a) Modification by irregular denting Some special reeds do not have evenly-spaced wires (see Figure 1). Existing reeds can be adapted by removing wires to create larger dents. This enables a variety of thickness of thread to be used in a warp and was almost certainly the method used to handweave the 1930s Rodier dress fabric shown on page 94, where a thick and irregular handspun woollen yarn is used in conjunction with fine wool crêpe yarns. (The same combination would have been simple to achieve weftways, but would not have draped well as a dress fabric.)

'Special effect' reeds have been produced from time to time: often for leno weaving and related cloths. They were based on the fact that a wire need not go from baulk to baulk, but could bridge over others and return to the same baulk. Threads entered in those dents could be transferred to another position during weaving.

In making reeds, any material used must be strong and smooth. If a coarse reed is being made, the thickness of the material is not crucial.

1 Cotton, spaced warp and weft. Threads held in place by hem-stitching. Pre-Columbian Peru. (Larry Edman Collection)
2 Furnishing fabric with warp bands of double density, concealing weft stripes which can then appear as blocks. (Jane Reeves, West Surrey College of Art and Design, UK)
3 Cotton and silk fabric, sett at double density in the twill bands. (Alison Kingsbury, West Surrey College of Art and Design, UK)

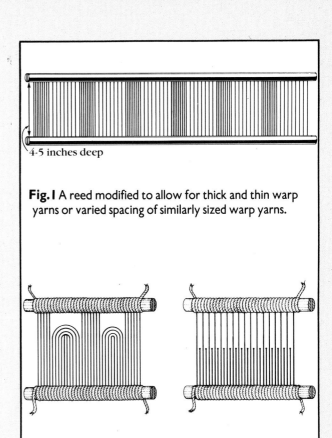

4-5 inches deep

Fig.1 A reed modified to allow for thick and thin warp yarns or varied spacing of similarly sized warp yarns.

Fig.2 Reeds modified to allow for changing positions of warp yarns.

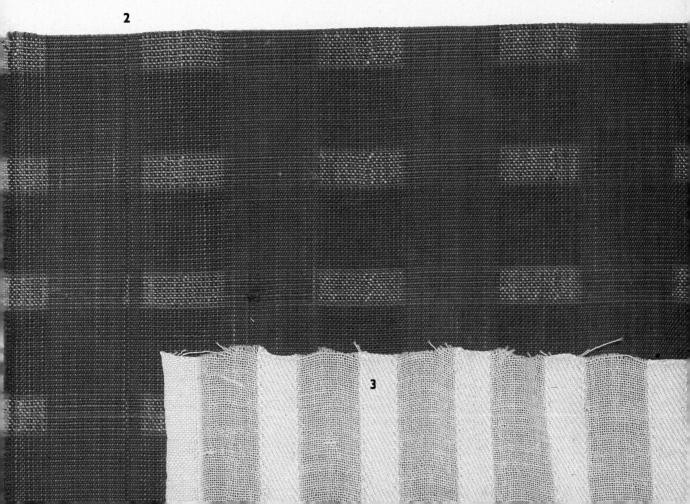

2

3

b) Modification by wire angle Usually, wires are set vertically between the reed baulks, but they can also be set at fanning angles. These are known as 'ondulé' reeds, and are much deeper between baulks than conventional reeds. During weaving the warp threads move gradually from a spaced position to a crammed, and back again. The resulting cloth is known as 'warp-way ondulé'.

Small, fan-shaped reeds were used industrially at the turn of the century for making slipper uppers, and for other small, shaped pieces.

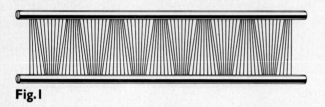

Fig.1

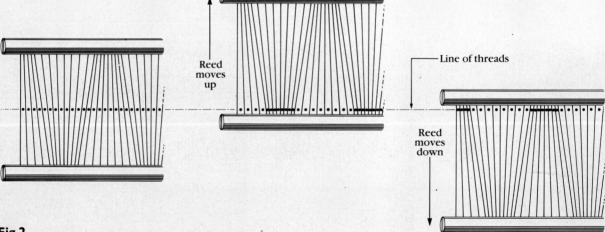

Fig.2

Right: Placemat with ondulé cotton warp and rigid weft. Far East, c.1960.

Inset right: Ondulé reed. Japan. (Photo by Diane Sheehan)

Fig.1 Ondulé reed structure.

Fig.2 Control of warp spacing by the upward and downward motion of an ondulé reed.

c) Modification by reed profile When the beating function of the reed is considered, the normal flat surface presented by the reed to the fell of the cloth becomes a possibility for modification. Profiled reeds, where the upper baulk is curved in opposition to the lower baulk, are slowly raised and lowered during weaving in the same way, presenting a slight change of profile with every beat.

These modifications result in fabrics with a waved-weft appearance, known as 'weft-ondulé'. (A simpler way to produce a similar effect is to use an alternating-tension device — see page 104.)

d) Modification by division of reed length By dividing the reed into smaller units, and fastening these side by side into the batten, it becomes possible to transpose sections of warp during weaving. This is the basis of the modification which Peter Collingwood employs to create his 'Macrogauze' hangings (see page 102).

Right: **Fig.1** Warp/weft ondulé reed.

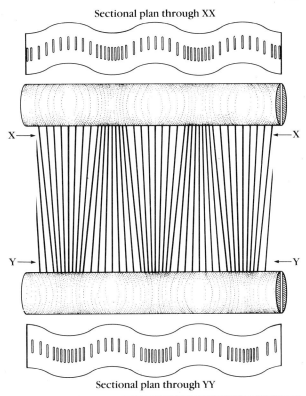

Sectional plan through XX

X →   ← X

Y →   ← Y

Sectional plan through YY

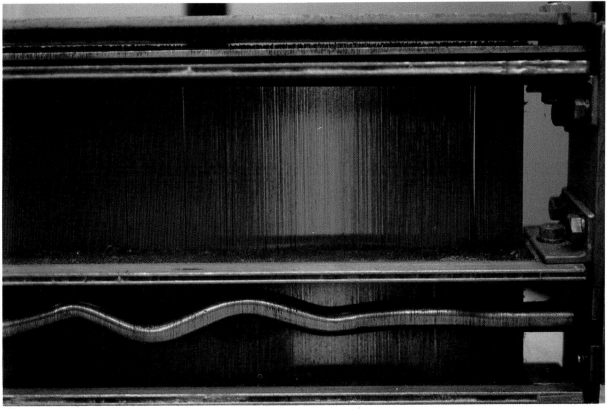

Left:
A combination of warp-ondulé and weft-ondulé is possible in the same fabric. In a hanging woven by Watabun Company in the Nishijin area of Kyoto, both warp and weft bands are seen to widen and narrow. It is possible that this was achieved by the use of a warp/weft ondulé reed, in which the wires were fanned and where the baulks were profiled also. (Photo John Markley)

Above:
A reed seen in Japan has no top baulk: the long and mobile wires are pushed into wave formation by a curved steel rod, activated by cams. The beating surface of the reed can therefore be contoured in many different ways during weaving. (Photo by Diane Sheehan)

101

Macrogauze

Peter Collingwood (UK) has invented a technique which frees the warp from the usual limitations of remaining parallel to itself and the selvedges. In his 'Macrogauze' series of hangings, the bands of linen warp lie at various angles. He achieves this by replacing the usual shafts and reed with a number of narrow rigid heddles housed side by side in a specially-constructed batten. Each rigid heddle is threaded with a separate warp which is wound on a weighted bobbin and hung over the back of the loom. The batten is on springs, and can move up and down to provide the sheds. The rigid heddles can be moved apart or together, or crossed over each other to provide elaborate variations on the gauze weave theme.

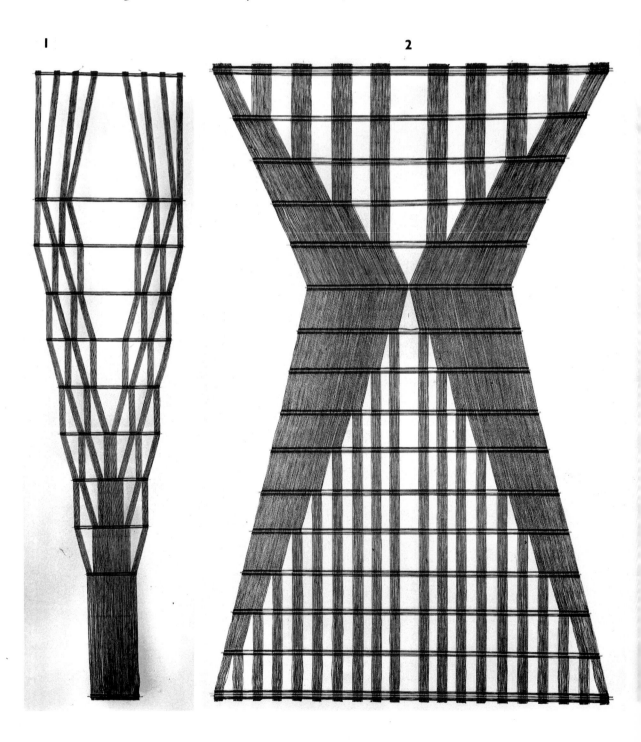

1

2

1 Peter Collingwood (UK): 'Macrogauze 19', 100 in × 24 in (254 cm × 61 cm), Linen.
2 Peter Collingwood (UK): 'Macrogauze 33', 60 in × 40 in (152 cm × 102 cm), Linen.
3 Peter Collingwood (UK): 'Macrogauze 35', 84 in × 20 in (213 cm × 51 cm), Linen.

4 Peter Collingwood (UK): 'Macrogauze 56', 87 in × 37 in (221 cm × 94 cm), Linen.
5 Peter Collingwood (UK): 'Macrogauze 64', 87 in × 33 in (221 cm × 84 cm), Linen.

(All photos by Charles Seely)

3 4 5

Tension Control

The recommended tension for the warp is usually 'even', and this is another rule which can be questioned to advantage. When the warp is accidentally uneven in tension, then the fell appears to waver and the resulting cloth is undulating and downgraded. It is worth considering the possibilities of 'controlled' uneven tension, and how it can be achieved. Excessive variation in tension needs two warp beams, and is therefore dealt with on page 110. Slight tensioning and relaxing in a warp can produce dramatic effects on any type of loom.

The simplest way to achieve this is to insert a rod (broomstick handle or similar) under the selected groups of threads to be tensioned, and push it to the back of the loom. After a few picks have been inserted, the rod can be reinserted under different groups of threads. The results will

be areas in the cloth where the weft has beaten down more than in others, so building up solid colour or texture.

A more efficient way to produce regular effects would be to carry bands of warp ends over or under two parallel rods which are fastened together at the ends. This frame can be tipped up and down by means of cords attached to spare pedals, and the bands of warp can be tensioned and relaxed during weaving (see Fig. 1).

Where individual bands need to be weighted heavily during weaving, they can have weights added at the back. Some weavers find that large plastic bottles with handles make ideal weights as they are infinitely controllable by filling with water to the required weight.

It is easy to convert all floor looms to the friction brake control which gives an automatic self-releasing tension to the back beam, with the resulting benefit that advancing the

warp is merely a matter of winding the cloth on to the cloth beam. Two ropes wind around the ends of the warp beam weighted individually at one end, but jointly weighted by a box at the other. This box can contain any weights, such as rocks, to produce the tension required. The box should be suspended as close to the floor as possible (see Fig. 2). The ratchet and pawl should not be removed for this conversion, merely thrown out of action temporarily. The tension obtained will be found to be elastic, and responsive to the beater. It will not be firm enough for rug-weaving, but will improve the quality of, for example, a woollen dress-weight cloth.

It is possible to use the qualities of differential warp tension without any devices, merely by using elastic and non-elastic yarns, which will relax at different rates off the loom.

Tucked cotton cloth, pressed. (Janet Oliver, Royal College of Art, UK: West Surrey College of Art and Design Collection)

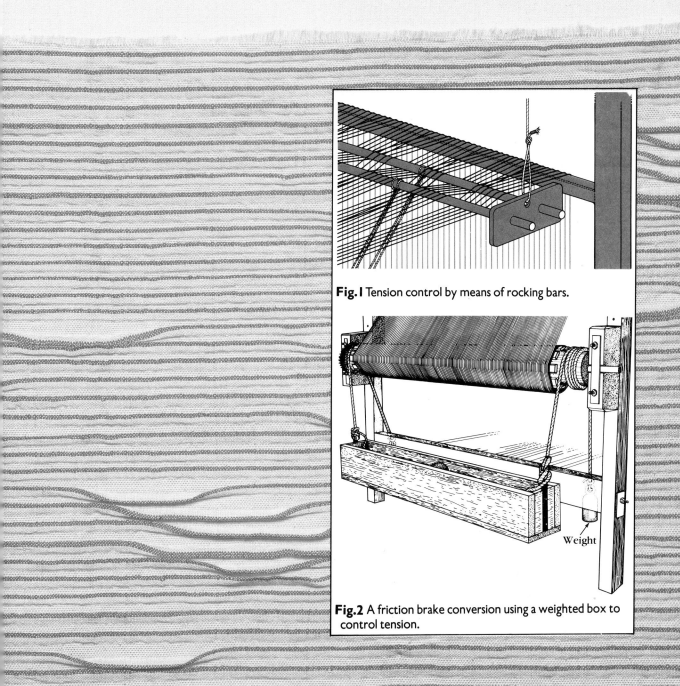

Fig. 1 Tension control by means of rocking bars.

Weight

Fig. 2 A friction brake conversion using a weighted box to control tension.

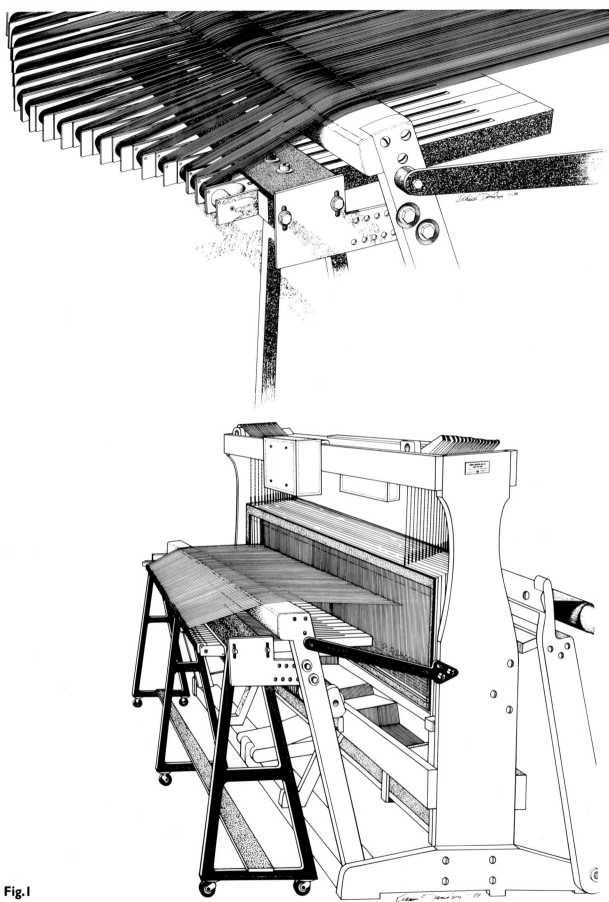

Fig.I

Special Devices

In developing her own weave vocabulary, Janice Lessman-Moss of Kent, Ohio, broke one of the cardinal rules of even tension maintenance. A number of discontinuous wefts of very dissimilar diameters and lengths (including painted and wrapped dowel rods) were used across the width of the weaving, building up in masses of colour and textural change. The variation in take-up caused such extreme tension problems that she had to decide whether to accede to the limitations of the loom and change her way of working, or try to modify the tool (the loom) to make it work for her.

With grants from the Ohio Arts Council and Kent State University, and with the aid of machinist/designer John Steinert, she developed a tensioning device, reminiscent of a type used on the eighteenth-century silk velour looms described by Diderot. One-inch units of warp pass around corresponding one-inch wide spools attached to sliding bars.

When the weaving begins all the sliding bars are fully retracted, but as the tension becomes maladjusted, the weaver can take up slack by sliding the appropriate bars out using a special tool which allows access between the stretched warps. The bars are then locked in their new positions and the weaving can continue until a new adjustment must be made. Re-tensioning a 72 in. wide warp can take five to ten minutes.

Although automation of the tensioning would improve the design, this pioneering, problem-solving spirit is an important first step in the creation of a new option for the loom. Communication between the problem-setter and the problem-solver worked here to allow the loom to change according to the weaver's needs. More work like this would bring the handweaving loom (which suffers from innovation deprivation) out of rustic technology and into the twentieth century.

Left:
Fig.1 The tensions of one-inch wide bands of warp can be controlled separately by this device on the back of Janice Lessman Moss's loom.

1 Cut and uncut velvet of metal and silk. Italy, 15th century. (Larry Edman Collection)
2 Cut and figured pile on chiffon ground. Silk. France, c.1920s.
3 Handwoven velvet with resist-dyed silk pile. (Elizabeth Milner, West Surrey College of Art and Design, UK)

2

3

Two Warp Beams

The addition of an extra warp beam (or two) to a loom enables the weaver to release warp ends at two or more different rates, often with dramatic results. If it is impractical to add an extra warp beam as a permanent addition to the loom, a satisfactory result can be obtained by backing up another loom to the one on which the cloth is to be woven, and securing it firmly. (This solution is used even by industry.) The extra beams which can be added in this way are, in theory, limited only by the number of looms available.

Traditional fabrics which have been woven with the help of two or more warp beams include velvet, seersucker and tucked cloth.

Velvet Velvet is commonly defined as a warp-pile fabric in which an extra warp is run over a series of small rods, which raise the threads over the base fabric. (*Velveteen* is a short-pile fabric in which the pile is formed by cutting the weft threads after weaving; *plush* has a long warp-pile and is loosely woven; *moquette* is a velvet in which the pile is made of wool or mohair on a cotton ground.)

Where the ground is entirely covered with pile the velvet is described as 'solid'. When some areas are free of pile, it is called 'voided velvet'. In 'uncut velvet' the warp loops are left uncut. Many elaborate Jacquard velvets include cut and uncut velvet figuring, often on a satin ground. The pile may

be of several different lengths, and both pile and voids may contain metallic threads, often brocaded.

Common velvet structures range from fine dress weight, through upholstery moquettes, to Wilton carpets. All use the same method of forming a pile on the surface of the cloth, but different materials make the cloths suitable for the different end uses. Until 1750, velvets were made of filament silk, and its light-reflective properties made the cloth seem alive with colour, with deep shadows and bright highlights accentuated by draping. The yarn chosen for the pile will always dictate the character of the cloth: a firm two-ply yarn will stand upright, a soft spun yarn will lie flat.

To weave plain velvet, two warps are needed, each on a separate beam preferably with friction tension. One of these is for the ground warp, which may be woven as plain weave, twill or satin, and the other is the pile warp. The pile warp must be made between five and twelve times the length of the ground warp (depending on the depth of the pile). The ground warp is often three or four times denser than the pile warp.

A special cloth beam is necessary if any length of velvet is to be woven: this is hollow, and allows the velvet to travel round an inner core to maintain tension, and to emerge without being crushed. An alternative is for the reverse of the cloth to pass over a friction roller, and then straight into a box.

Cut and uncut single colour velvet. Probably China, c. 1890. (Larry Edman Collection)

One or two shafts, for the pile warp, are hung close to the reed, with the ground warp passing through as many of the other shafts as the weave requires.

In weaving, all the pile ends are lifted, and a rod inserted. This is made of wood or, for fine work, smooth metal, often brass, and it has a groove running along the top edge. Two or three ground picks are inserted, then another pile rod, and this is repeated until between six and twelve rods are in place. Then the cutting begins: a sharp blade is drawn down the groove of the rod which was inserted first. This cuts the pile and releases the rod, which is then inserted at the fell again. The number of rods in the cloth must be maintained to prevent the pile from being pulled flat under tension. An alternative method is to use rods which have a small blade built in to the far end, so that the loops are cut as the rod is withdrawn. Uncut velvet is woven by withdrawing the rods in the same way, but without cutting the pile. Rows can consist of part cut, part uncut pile.

Velvet is usually woven commercially by weaving two fabrics face-to-face, with a pile warp passing from one cloth to the other. The two cloths are cut apart on the loom before being stored on two cloth beams.

Handwoven velvet is rarely produced today; an exception being the weaving of velvet for Coronation robes in Britain. Luther Hooper noted in *Handloom Weaving* that: 'One yard of velvet is about a day's work for a good weaver'.

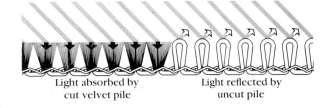

Fig.1 Light reflecting qualities of cut and uncut velvet pile.

Light absorbed by cut velvet pile

Light reflected by uncut pile

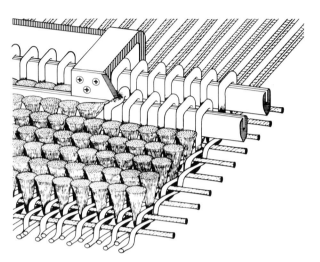

Fig.2 Two velvet fabrics woven face to face.

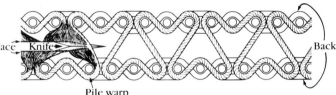

Face   Knife   Back

Pile warp

Fig.3 The structure and cutting of velvet pile.

Seersucker (from the Persian 'shirushaker': milk and sugar). Another dramatic use of two warp beams is in the weaving of a familiar fabric, seersucker, in which alternating bands of warp are woven at ordinary and slack tensions, producing permanently crinkled stripes.

This tensioning is most effective in closely woven cloths, with narrow bands of seersucker. During weaving, at least one of the two beams should be controlled by a friction brake, and the most definite effect is obtained by the use of an 'easer bar', which holds the slack warp at a tension only during the forming of the shed, slackening it again as the weft is beaten into place.

There are other ways of producing a warpways puckered stripe:

1. by the use of two yarns which will shrink differently during the finishing process;
2. using overspun yarns for alternate stripes.

These can also be used to produce weft seersucker, and so, of course, crinkle checks.

It is interesting to compare the length of threads pulled from the different stripes of a seersucker cloth, to realize the difference needed in the warp lengths.

Seersucker should not be confused with *plissé*, where the crinkle stripes are caused by an application of caustic soda (see page 152).

1 Seersucker of plain weave and hopsack bands. Mercerized cotton. (Brigit Jackson, West Surrey College of Art and Design, UK)
2 Silk and wool seersucker with irregular take-up. (Roger Thorpe, West Surrey College of Art and Design, UK)
3 Tucked and pressed cloth. (Janet Oliver, Royal College of Art, UK: West Surrey College of Art and Design Collection)
4 Weft tucks in silk and cotton, padded with nylon. (Alison M. Ellen, West Surrey College of Art and Design, UK)

4

3

2

1

2

'86 KEIKO KOBAYASHI

PROCESS AND PRODUCT

Early in the nineteenth century an ingenious Glasgow weaver, David Anderson by name, wove several remarkable things upon his loom. Among them he made a shirt, with a fine frill, double-stitched neck, shoulder straps, and wrist bands, with gussets, buttons, buttonholes, and the Royal Arms emblazoned on the breast, which he presented to King George IV. Whoever attentively studies the loom will perceive that the famous shirt was not a mere freak of genius, but is only one of the many things which might be woven, if due encouragement were given to enterprise in that direction. But the weaver is required to produce, for the most part, only cloths which may be fashioned into garments or other useful commodities. – William S. Murphy, *The Textile Industries,* 1911.

Weavers are rightly preoccupied with skill and craftsmanship. As in other practical subjects, the processes must be mastered before they can be reconsidered. A high level of attainment in skill is, of course, admired, but it does not in itself lead to the production of fascinating cloth. When the skilled maker starts to apply ingenuity to the processes, the cloth seems to acquire the excitement generated by the discoveries made. Almost every basic procedure in weaving is capable of being questioned, and the results may be time-saving or spectacular, often both. Often the investigation will result in the same brainwave which hit another weaver, even centuries before, but occasionally the idea is original. When a 'process' discovery is linked with fresh thinking, in only one other direction, the weaver has a personal direction which could involve a lifetime's investigation.

The Warp

Variations on warp colour, texture, size and sett have occupied the thoughts of weavers. There are, however, other possibilities for the experienced weaver to consider. Pre-Columbian weavers created cloths in which warps as well as wefts were discontinuous. Unlike tapestry, these are lightweight fabrics of nearly balanced weave in which distinct colour changes in both warp and weft are made possible by interlocking threads. The cloths were made on frame looms with temporary 'scaffolding' threads (perhaps even loosely woven cloth) as structural support during warping and weaving.

1 Interlocking warp and weft, wool. Pre-Columbian, probably Nazca. Peru. (Larry Edman Collection)
2 Keiko Kobayashi: Interlocked warp and weft. Japan, 1986.

1

Discontinuous Warps

Are there any other cases in which warps are not continuous from the beginning to the end of the weaving process? Any weaver who has experienced the frustration of broken warp ends knows how to replace one. Taking this knowledge one step beyond mere *necessity*, one might use the *opportunity* to change the colour, size or texture of a thread by the same technique. The result might be similar to that of resist-dyed warp if the same type of thread were used, but more distinctive changes may be possible with changes in texture or fibre types. Thinking one step further: while the warp is disengaged from the loom, could the threading of that warp change so the weave might be dramatically affected? (Empty heddles may be left anywhere within the width of the warp or clip-on heddles are available for the same result.)

Peter Collingwood has evolved an efficient shaft-switching device, in which ends can be transferred from one shaft to another by means of a keyboard of levers at eye level. This enables him to create elaborate blockweave patterning in his rugs.

It is up to the weaver to *test* the idea, making certain that the result cannot be achieved more efficiently and that the effect is worth the extra cost and effort.

1 Warp threads replaced to simulate an ikat effect. (Ann Richards, West Surrey College of Art and Design, UK)
2 Linen damask napkin. The green ends and picks outlining the central grid are clipped off to remove them from the border pattern. 20th century (UK)
3 By linking two different coloured threads, starting at either end, each warp can change colour dramatically at some point in the weave. Care must be taken when threading to avoid 'locks' of warp during weaving: the ends must be selected in the correct pairs. (Ann Sutton)

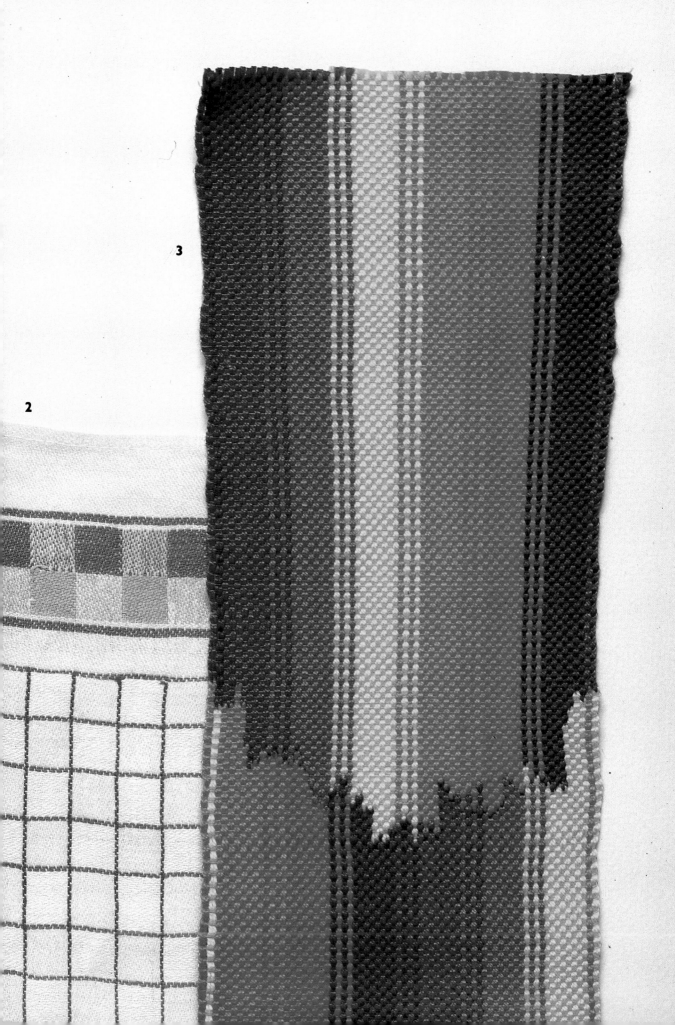

2

3

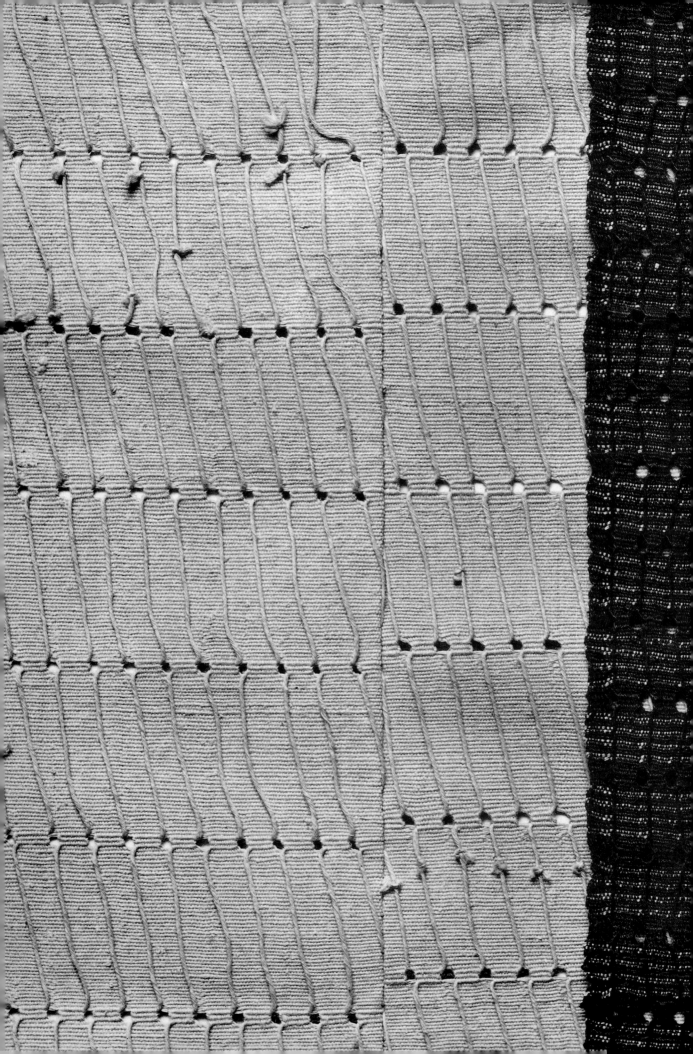

Transposing Warp and Weft

In handweaving, the traditional roles of warp and weft threads can be questioned. Warps can be woven with themselves: the triangular shawl, already popular with handweavers, is an ingenious example where a short warp, often filling the complete width of the loom, is cut at the back, end after end from one side, drawn through to the front and used in turn as weft. The result is a triangle with a selvedge along the hypotenuse and fringes on the two short edges — an ideal structure for a shawl, and one which wastes almost no material.

It is interesting to reverse this thinking: weft can become warp, so that a minimum number of warp threads is supplemented by extended picks which, once woven into the cloth, are then threaded through reed and healds to the rear of the loom.

Taking this further: weft could become warp and then could be used as weft again. In cloth woven by the Yoruba in Nigeria, traditionally used as clothing, ventilation is important. Permanent holes are created during weaving by taking extra wefts to and fro over short areas of warp, pulling hard to create gaps in the cloth, which is then woven conventionally for a few inches until another row of holes is required, when the same extra wefts are brought back into action. The diagonal floats of the extra wefts appear to be warpwise, and form a decorative element to this functional cloth, travelling vertically or at an angle, depending on the side chosen for the next insertion.

Cotton, transposed warp/weft. Strip weave. Yoruba. Nigeria, 1970.

Selvedges

The selvedge (literally: 'self-edges'), is probably the most talked-about element in the handweaver's cloth. It is especially problematic for beginners, and is the traditional inspection point for good craftsmanship. Indeed, properly woven selvedges are essential to good cloth and their attainment has been written about extensively. For an area of the cloth which is paid so much technical attention, very little consideration has been given to the *possibilities* of the selvedge (except in industrial weaving, where fancy effects or brand names are sometimes incorporated).

It is well-known that the *tension* of selvedges can be controlled, often to the extent of providing separate bobbins for their warps. Taken to extremes, this could produce tight edges with slack central cloth area, or slack edges to the cloth looking like frills.

The *position* of the selvedge can be considered: it can be the leading edge in viewing the fabric, or extra selvedges can be woven as features (extensions) in the body of the cloth.

The selvedge can be accentuated by colour and/or yarn or woven as a tube (which could be the means of housing another element). Pieces of cloth can be woven with selvedges round all four sides: this is nearly impossible on a conventional loom, but a comparatively simple operation on a backstrap loom. (The process is described well in *Backstrap Weaving* by Barbara Taber and Marilyn Anderson.)

Extended Selvedges The 'rule' of straight selvedges can be broken to good effect by deliberately extending the edge of a cloth in areas, so that the weft provides a profile. Obviously, this is most effective when there is a minimum width of fabric between the selvedges, so the technique is used traditionally in ribbon-making. The selvedges on ribbons and braids are prominent, and can be an important element in the design. They must still provide firm straight edges, for durability; different weaves, contrasting colours, and extended edge loops or picots, have all been used by the ribbon industry to decorate their fabrics. Of these, the extended edge is one of the most dramatic effects, and one which has many untapped possibilities.

The effect can be achieved by including 'false warps' as selvedges, called 'catch cords', which are used to control the extension of the weft only to degrees beyond the edge of the ground fabric, and withdrawing them when the weaving is complete. These can be made of heavy thread or wire.

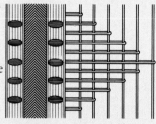

Fig. I Extended selvedges by use of 'false warps'.

The specialized area of weaving called *passementerie* (decorative braids, fringes and tassels) has involved many ingenious methods of extending both edges of narrow trimmings with false warps, templates and weft yarns which are deliberately overspun in order that they can twist together into bunches when they are released into fringes.

1 Trimming ribbon with space-dyed weft: extended selvedges. Contemporary.
2 Passamenterie: silk. Cut and uncut extended selvedges. 19th century.
3 Scaffolded cloth, subsequently tie-dyed. Extended warp edge loops are formed by groups of 6 warp yarns which twist together to make a loop around a first or last weft. Pre-Columbian Peru. (Larry Edman Collection)

3

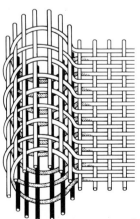
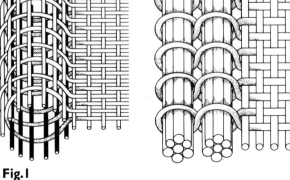

Detail of neckpiece by Diane Sheehan 1977.
Weft extends to form a hinge which joins narrow strips of double-cloth and warp-repp silk and lurex fabric. (Photo by Diane Sheehan. Diane Itter Collection)

Fig. 1 Two possible selvedge modifications which might enhance the structural or aesthetic qualities of the cloth. On the left a selvedge woven as a tube and on the right multiple yarns used as selvedge warps.

Fig.1

Working Selvedges Considering where the selvedge might occur and how it can be made to work in the finished object can result in economical as well as beautiful solutions. Contrary to the usual practice of removing selvedges before making-up cloth, leaving them on can provide the solution to many problems. They can carry the identity of the weaver; they can convolute the cloth after weaving; and they can eliminate the need for a stitched hem or other anti-fray device.

Model for a short boot by Salvador Ferragamo 1955/56,. The fabric is elasticized brocade of silk and lurex, used so that the selvedge produces a sturdy but beautiful frill around the top of the shoe. (Photo: Victoria and Albert Museum, London)

The Weft

Weaving involves the raising of certain warps to form a shed, picking or running a weft between these warps and beating or laying in the weft to determine its relative density in the cloth. The complexity of this operation and the fact that it is under the control of the weaver throughout the cloth-making process (as compared to the warp, which is customarily more predetermined) means that there are many opportunities for invention during this phase.

Weavers are often preoccupied with complicated weave structures, and consider themselves limited by numbers of shafts available, but hand-manipulations of the weft may be a great enhancement to loom-controlled weaves and, in fact, can be an advantage that the handweaver has over the mass-producer of cloth.

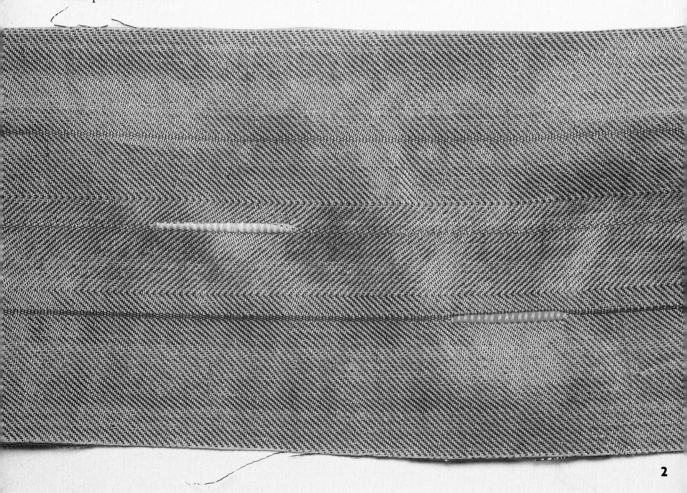

2

1 Placemat in which a design feature is made of the weft joins. Ramie. (Island Artcrafts Inc., Philippines)
2 Cotton warp, lurex weft, with chiffon rag inserts. (Lucy Coltman, West Surrey College of Art and Design, UK)

Black wefts are caught round an end at specific points and returned in the same shed; an increasing ratio of black to white ends creates a gradated colour-and-weave effect in the cloth. Cotton and linen. Holland, c.1980.

Shuttles

Shuttles come in all shapes and sizes, and at first sight do not seem to hold any possibilities for creativity in weaving, the majority being designed to perform a specific task: to hold a certain type of weft (e.g. ski shuttles for rug-weaving); or to release the weft with efficient control (e.g. fixed bobbin end-delivery shuttles).

At least one shuttle, however, can affect the appearance of the cloth when it is used. For example, the double-bobbin shuttle can hold two yarns of different texture and/or colour and leave the two wefts in the same shed without twisting, and at controlled tension. The alternative, of winding two yarns together on to the same pirn or bobbin, usually results in the yarns coming off at different tensions, with selvedge loops. On the other hand, it is possible to add twist when the two yarns are used on one pirn, by placing them so that one end runs up through the package of the other during winding. This can be effective in the cloth.

One of the biggest areas of development in the powerloom over the past few decades has been in the method of passing the weft through the shed. The invention of the flying-shuttle by John Kay in 1738 enabled wider cloth to be woven; towards the end of the nineteenth century it was proposed that shuttles could be guided by means of a magnet attracting the metal tip. It was also suggested that the warp threads could squeeze the tail of the shuttle to force it across, and, most importantly, that shuttles could be propelled by compressed air. More recently it was realized that shuttles were not necessary – the weft thread could be passed through the shed by means of rapiers, water jets or air. This enabled weaving to proceed at a faster rate, because it was no longer necessary to wind or load bobbins: the weft stands at the side of the loom on a large cone and is placed directly into the shed.

In today's looms, shuttles are used only by handweavers.

Overleaf:
Warp-print on black ground 'chameleon taffeta' which is given a shot effect by the placing of red and green picks sequentially in the same shed. Ribbon. France, 19th century.

Placing the Weft

Weavers carefully ensure that the batten on their loom is at exact right angles to the warp before starting to weave. This rule has been broken by both industry and the handweaver: woven wire sieve cloths, and special fabrics for balloons are both woven 'biased', with the weft at a 75-degree angle to the warp. Peter Collingwood, in his search for variations on plain weave fabrics, produced a series of linen 'Anglefell' hangings: first using the graded pivot positions on the loom to angle the weft from selvedge to selvedge, he later took the reed out of the batten and used it freely at judged angles to beat in triangular formation.

The reed can project a curved profile towards the fell by the simple insertion of a strip of plywood or stiff card, flat on the batten side and curved on the other, before beating.

Strong curved wire will perform the same function.

Beating the weft into place need not be done with any edge, straight or waved. When the threads are placed, a brush can be used to direct them to a position. A traditional Japanese hemp kimono fabric, *mizugoromo* or 'water cloth', uses a similar technique of weft placement. This technique is used today in Japan to make elaborately patterned silk obis. If the fabric is of narrow width, the weft can be placed with the fingers.

Another unconventional way of beating in the weft is practised in Japan today for fine tapestry-weaving: one edge of the fingernail of the middle finger of the right hand is finely notched, to beat in the silk weft without using any other tool.

Above:
Costume for an actor in the Noh theatre. Plain weave, with the weft beaten in irregularly. Bast fibre, starched. Japan, probably 19th century. (Honolulu Academy of Arts: No. 2211.1)
Left: Detail.

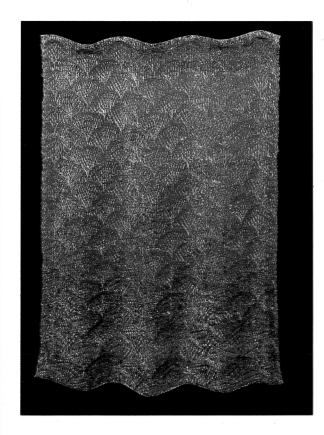

The Cloth

When a cloth leaves the loom it is hardly ever in a finished state. Most cloths need, at the very least, a light wash to close up, stabilize and often to soften, and to remove any dirt which might have accrued in the processes so far. Some types of cloth need severe finishing in order that the required qualities can be revealed, and some will leave the loom in a flat state but surfaces will eventually become three-dimensional as the fibres and yarns relax into the structure during a finishing process. A cloth in 'loom-state' often bears no resemblance to the same cloth after 'finishing'.

Practical finishing of small amounts of cloth has been well documented elsewhere. Little attention has been paid, however, to the creative possibilities of finishing processes. To be able to work in this area, the weaver must understand the properties of fibres when wet and dry, yarn twist and the relation of both of these to weave structure. To develop a creative attitude to cloth finishing, the conventional treatments should first be understood, and special attention given to any rules (which might later be broken to good effect).

Some finishes which are not often practised by the handweaver, and which have creative possibilities, are described on the following pages.

Above:
Lia Cook (USA): 'China Stage Curtain', 1985. Rayon, pressed in an etching press after weaving.
Left: Detail.

(Both photos by the artist)

1

2

Beetling

Of all the finishes applied to the woven textile, that of pressure, sometimes combined with heat and sometimes with excessive force, is the most common. The domestic task of 'ironing' aims to smooth out cloth with the aid of heated pressure (and sometimes moisture), and in Scandinavia the process of cold pressure on the damp cloth, in the form of a mangle, is considered vital to the maintenance of household linen. Linen (and some cotton) fabrics can be 'beetled' as part of the finishing process to enhance their lustre and smoothness, and in industry this is done with forty wooden hammers, each pounding the linen at 400 blows per minute in wet conditions. Originally this was done with a single heavy mallet or even a smooth stone.

In Africa, cotton cloth, heavily impregnated with indigo, is beetled until it resembles carbon paper, by two men who spit and beat in alternating rhythm, thus producing the ideal conditions for a lustrous and gleaming cloth.

In India, a mixture of lemon juice, sugar and water is used to soak silk cloth before it is rubbed with wooden paddles in order to 'add to the brilliance and set off fast colours'. This is followed by rubbing with the flat side of a hemispherical implement or beating with a mallet. In some areas, the wet silk is spread over a table and pressed with hot iron rods, giving a watery effect.

Pressing

Flat pressure, as opposed to the rollers of the calender (see page 136) is used in woollen and worsted manufacture where a firm finish is required. The cloth is interleaved with cardboard sheets, and put in a press. Heat is then applied. In Wales, woollen shawls are still finished in this way, with a fire being lit under the press.

1 Linen rug, beetled. (Angus Williams, West Surrey College of Art and Design, UK)
2,3 Linen and silk cloths, beetled. (Sue Gladwell, West Surrey College of Art and Design, UK)

3

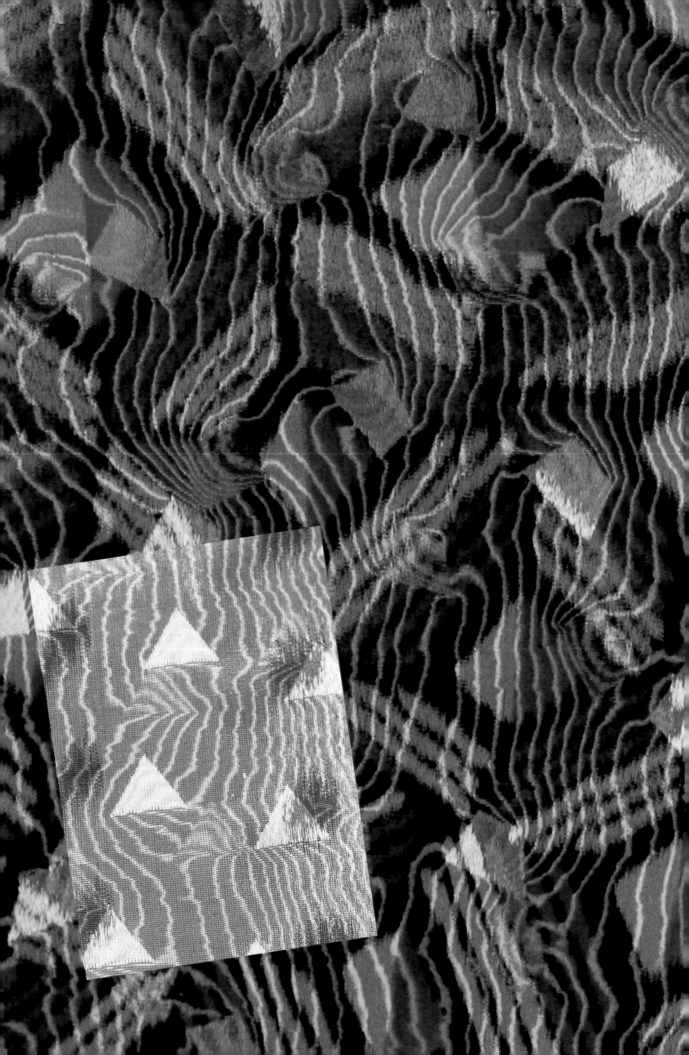

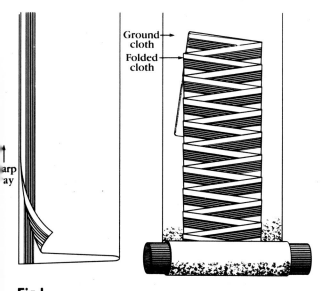

Fig. I

Calendering

Calendering is the industrial version of the domestic task of ironing. It is performed by running the cloth round alternate hard metal and softer cloth-wrapped, or solid paper rollers. Two metal rollers never run against one another.

The *Simple Calender* acts like the domestic iron (hard iron against soft ironing board). In the same way, it smoothes out wrinkles and gives a slight sheen.

The *Friction Calender* imparts a highly glazed surface. The cloth is soaked with starch and wax (for a temporary finish) or with resin (for a durable glaze) and *nearly* dried. The speed of one roller (metal) is faster than that of the cloth-covered one, and the resulting friction polishes the surface. If the metal is heated, a higher glaze is produced (see page 138 for 'Embossing'). A dramatic example of this finish is 'ciré', the brilliant polish which makes silk or rayon look like patent leather, produced by wax and hot calendering.

Issey Miyake has used a hot calendering process on synthetic fur fabric: the result looks like scaling leather.

Moire A very specialized process of calendering ribbed fabrics such as taffeta with reflective surfaces produces a 'watered' effect of faint and shimmering lines and 'eyes'. By folding the fabric in prescribed ways, the pronounced weftways ribs cross each other and are crushed under the pressure of calendering. These crushed threads reflect light differently from the surrounding area and so read as indistinct changes in colour and surface quality.

There are more than fifteen specific styles of French moire with elaborate techniques for achieving each. Some interesting processes include:

- the use of a ondulé reed to place the weft in waves so that when crossed and pressed sinuous lines are formed;
- having the woven cloth pass over a beam with bars in relief which cause the wefts to deviate and crush slightly while still on the loom;
- running the cloth through a calendering machine fitted with a roller with a heavily incised design so that the cloth is not crushed in certain areas, creating a specific pattern.

Strong pressure and intense heat are required to achieve the brilliance and change of surface necessary to create moiré effects.

Artists have been known to use unusual tools such as heavy road construction equipment and etching presses to transform woven surfaces.

1 and 2 Warp print, moiree. Silk. France, c. 1925. Musee Historique des Tissus, Lyons. (Photos Diane Sheehan)
Fig. I Diagram: One method of folding fabric before calendering, to produce moire effect.

Embossing

The *Embossing Calender* produces either flat or raised designs on the cloth. An engraved copper roller is heated, and presses the cloth against a smooth paper roll. Raised patterning is produced by soaking the paper roll in water and revolving it against the engraved metal roll until the pattern is impressed. The resulting male/female impression gives a distinct emboss to the cloth.

For handweavers, a carved wooden block should be placed right side up, with the cloth (usually silk) face side down on it. A damp press-cloth with a very hot iron, giving as much straight pressure as possible, should produce embossed patterning, which can be enhanced by rubbing the dry iron directly on to the silk while it is still on the block. This embossing cannot be washed, but should withstand dry-cleaning.

Slashing

In the sixteenth and seventeenth centuries, plain silk cloth was often made to look more expensive by embossing designs in order to reflect light from the relief areas. This embossing process would sometimes cut through the precious handwoven fabric, and it is possible that out of such disasters the idea of slashing the cloth in a decorative way was born. It became an accepted and fashionable way to embellish a fabric, and cuts (which could be straight or with pinked edges to avoid fraying) gave life and pattern to a plain silk surface. A later development was to pull areas of an under-fabric through the slashes in the top cloth, to form decorative puffs of contrasting colour.

Embossed and slashed satins, c. 16th century. (Victoria and Albert Museum, London. Nos. 746-1894 and 835-1901)

Cutting

The sight of finely woven silk slashed and frayed at the edges should coax handweavers out of a protective attitude to the cloth they weave. The effects of cutting and washing on a simply structured fabric can be surprising and enhancing. Rae Chalmers (USA) weaves yards of plain woven cloth with great speed. Cutting this cloth on the bias and interlacing the resulting strips, she makes a double thick but supple fabric. The soft cotton yarns, pre-dyed by the weaver, are encouraged to fray during washing and drying to produce a diagonal grid of fringes across the surface. The finished cloth, much more interesting than its original form, is ideally suited for the end product: distinctive jackets.

Rae Chalmers (USA): Cut and interwoven cloth.
Cotton. 1987.

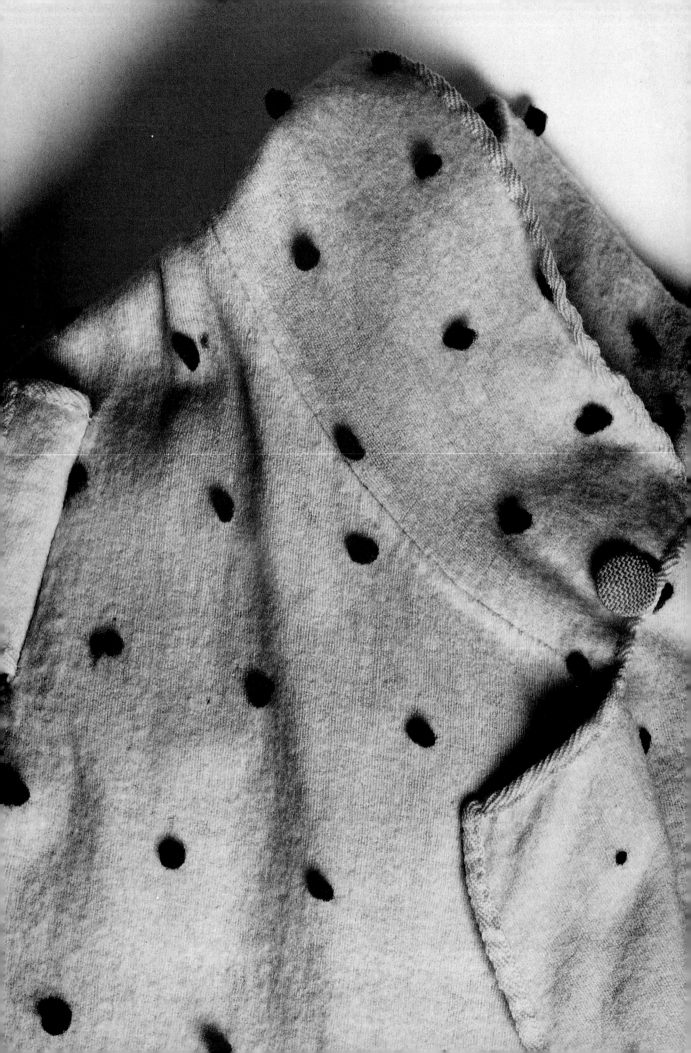

Fulling

The finishing process known as fulling, or milling, depends on the felting property of wool fibres. The cloth, often limp and open, is subjected to extensive mechanical action in soapy water. Originally this was done with the pressure of feet, in a tub, and the aid of 'fuller's earth'. Later, pounding wooden hammers, often powered by fast-running streams, performed the same function. Today, in Greece, the well-known flokati rugs, woven with tufts of wool inserted into a cloth base, are laid at the base of a waterfall, where the pounding water felts the fibres and holds the rug together.

If cloth is milled or fulled for a long time, the weave can be completely obscured by a felt-like surface, and the cloth will have shrunk considerably, becoming much thicker. In tailoring a wool cloth, this property is used to shrink out excess fullness.

A cloth destined for milling should be woven with an open sett in a soft twist single or two-ply yarn. Sewing the selvedges together to form a tube has been found to prevent them waving during the process. Some weavers full their cloth in a washing machine with a hot wash and a cold rinse, including bath towels in the load to give friction. Tumble-drying will give an even thicker cloth, and shrink it further.

Overleaf:
Cotton warp, wool weft. The weaves chosen for adjacent areas have very different intersection ratios. The subsequent wet finishing and hot drying in motion cause uneven shrinkage to occur, resulting in a three-dimensional cloth. 1987. (Junichi Arai, Japan)

Left:
Tufts of black wool inserted during the weaving are held in place by fulling, to imitate ermine. Nightgown, English 1815-22, worn by Thomas Coutts (Victoria and Albert Museum, London. Circ.718/7-1912)

Below:
Wool roving is floated in blocks and felted to the base weave. (Ann Richards, West Surrey College of Art and Design, UK)

1 Teasels used for raising cloth. One is trimmed ready for insertion into a raising machine.
2 Pet-grooming brush suitable for hand-raising.
3 Leonardo da Vinci: Drawing of proposed cloth-raising machine. 14.57 in × 9.65 in (37 cm × 24.5 cm). It shows his idea of fixed teasels and moving cloth, as opposed to the conventional method of the time. (Ambrosiana Library, Milan)

Raising

Raising (also called Gigging, Napping or Brushing) – the process of lifting fibres out of a cloth so that they lie on one or both surfaces – is one of the oldest of the finishing operations. Traditionally, it is applied to blankets (the extra layer of loose fibres providing insulation) and to fine surfaced wool cloths such as billiard cloth, where the raised surface is subsequently cropped (see page 150) to give an extra smooth finish. Raising has, for centuries, been done with the dried heads of teasels (*Dipsacus fullonum* or Fuller's Thistle) which were originally mounted in a handheld frame, and later on the surface of a cylinder. Even today, the finest raising still uses the sensitive teasel heads, but most have been replaced by card clothing (as on the hand cards used to prepare fibres for spinning).

All cloth can be raised to a greater or lesser extent. The combination of cloth type, fibre quality and conditions of raising will determine the effect. Slow speeds produce the most even pile; if a blanket-like surface is required, the cloth is raised dry, but if the pile is required to lie down, it is raised in a wet condition.

For the handweaver, raising is most effective while the cloth is under tension on the loom. A small hand card (often sold for pet-grooming) is ideal and it should be dragged firmly *across* the fabric, from selvedge to selvedge, so that the position of the weft threads is not affected (the warp is kept in place by tension). Only the last few strokes must be made warpways, if that is the intended direction of the pile. Only one side of the cloth can be brushed in this way, and an area can be treated every time the cloth is advanced in the loom.

It should be noted that some yarns are designed to be raised: the familiar brushed mohair scarves are woven with a yarn in which the mohair is looped on the surface. These loops are intended to be broken out during the raising process, to give maximum cover of fibres. The 'brushed mohair' yarn used by knitters was originally looped, but has been raised in the yarn stage, and, when used in weaving, will not raise as well as the loop variety.

In the UK, *napping* refers to a separate finishing process: that of rubbing a raised and cropped fabric between a rubber and a plush sheet, in controllable movements. This gives a pilled or ridged surface to the cloth, often seen in overcoats.

Overleaf:
1 Cropping was used in the removal of unwanted weft floats from the reverse of Paisley shawls in the early 19th century. The many coloured yarns necessary for these elaborate designs resulted in floats in between the surface appearances, which were cut away afterwards, giving the characteristic furry back to the cloth. (The waste was later worked up into carpets.)
2 Cloqué spots in wool worsted (crêpe and regular yarns). Surplus white yarns are clipped away after weaving. Probably France, c.1920.
3 Coloured areas of double cloth are isolated on a white ground by clipping away the floats on the reverse. Wool. (Rosemary Tomlinson, West Surrey College of Art and Design, UK)

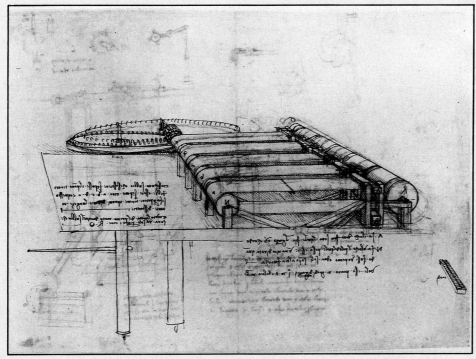

3

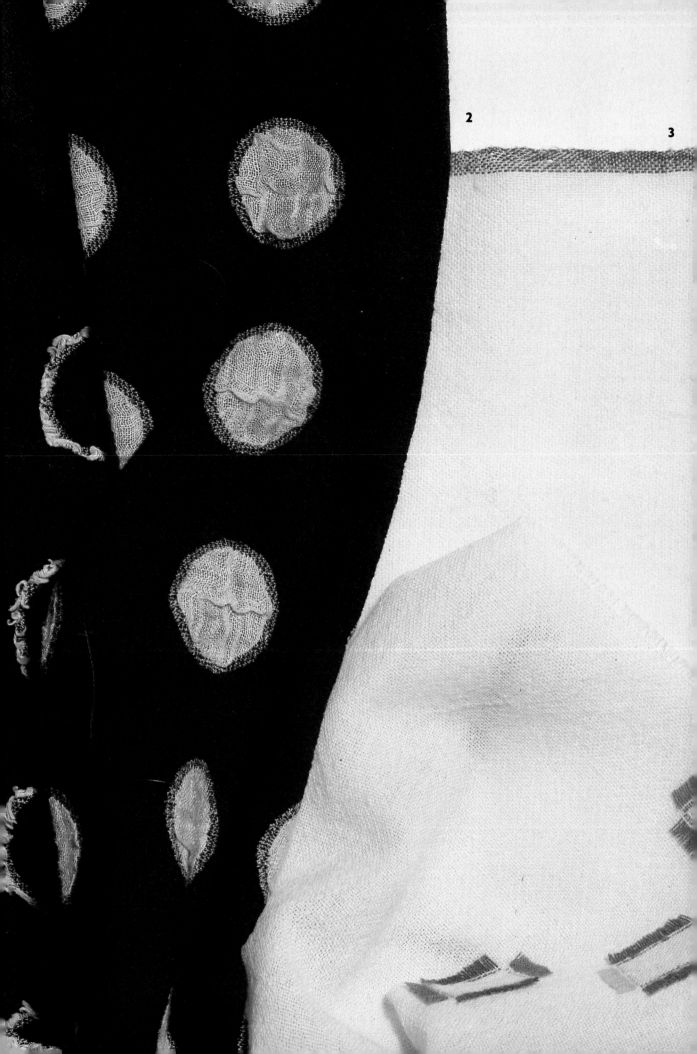

2

3

1 Cotton and silk diagonal corduroy, floats cut before washing. (Barbara Munns, West Surrey College of Art and Design, UK)
2 Spun silk vertical and diagonal corduroy. Cut and steamed in finishing. (Susie Lees, West Surrey College of Art and Design, UK)

Cropping

Because of the traditional preference for smooth cloth, it has become customary to crop the surface of many wool cloths as a final finishing process. The cloth is passed under a rotating roller bearing blades set spirally, like a lawn mower. Even fabrics which have been raised are given a light cropping to even the surface. The process is also applied to tweeds, and even fine worsted cloths. It is essential for 'face cloths' and velours, in which successive raising and cropping produces a matt surface with no apparent weave.

Sometimes these cloths are then patterned by cutting a design into the surface. This is done by passing the cloth over a roller which has the design in relief, usually in copper strip. The cropping blades cut only the areas which are pushed up by the wires.

Clipping

When extra threads are used as a small area of colour and/or texture in a cloth, they can either be woven into the body of the cloth between appearances, or they can float loosely on the back or front, and subsequently be cut away. These threads can be in the warp, weft or both, and are almost always extra to the background structure (so that their total removal would leave a plain cloth). The fact that the extra threads are crammed into the reed along with the background structure helps to nip them firmly into the cloth for the areas where they weave in.

The way in which the threads are clipped can vary. The surplus thread can be removed completely or cut to hang on the surface. It can be cut straight or at an angle, very close to the woven area, or with a residual fringe. These fringes can be finished so that they fall in any chosen direction.

On page 30, Randall Darwall's handwoven scarf shows an effective use of clipped fringing. Extra threads in the warp are floated and woven in, then clipped at angles and brushed in one direction before pressing to form a rich silk surface which he describes as 'laciniated'. The fringes change direction in the centre of the scarf so that each end strokes downwards.

Corduroy, along with the weft face *velveteen,* depends on clipping for its character: weft floats are clipped in warpwise wales, and the cut ends are then burst during finishing into the familiar furry surface.

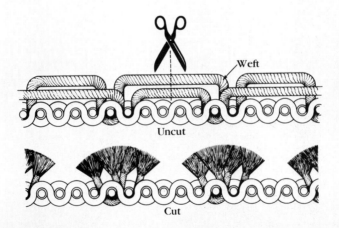

Uncut

Cut

Fig. I The structure and clipping of corduroy (section through warp).

Chemical Treatments

Although many of the chemical finishes for textiles are beyond the scope of handweavers, it is worth considering the effects which certain chemicals have on the various fibres, and how they can be used to advantage on a smaller scale. For example, the familiar process of *starching* in order to stiffen cotton during laundering: during the vogue for shiny collars, this finish was achieved by rapidly polishing the starched surface with a hot iron. This is the equivalent to the 'calendering', which a glazed chintz will undergo.

Some chemicals which produce visible effects on fibres are:

- on cotton a crisp parchment effect is produced by the application of strong *sulphuric acid,* carefully controlled and timed (five to six seconds). The cloth is then neutralized by washing in a weak alkali. It can then be calendered. (This is the finish used to produce organdie.) Another possibility with this process would be to paint areas with an acid-resisting substance before the cloth is run through acid. *Devoré* (burnt-out effects) is produced by applying sulphuric acid to a fabric which is woven with fibres from two different groups (e.g. rayon and silk). In this case the rayon is eaten away, and the silk remains.
- *Sodium hydroxide* (caustic soda) is the chemical used to mercerize cotton, to give it a silk-like lustre. This is applied when the cloth or yarn is stretched, and is a permanent finish. A solution of caustic soda is applied to cotton cloth, usually in warpways stripes. The treated parts shrink, causing the untreated stripes to puckers, in imitation of seersucker. This cloth is called '*plissé'*.
- Nylon will react in the same way if treated with *phenol*.
- Linen can be bleached with *hypochlorite, peroxide, sodium chlorite* (or even seven days of sunshine).
- Chinese carpets made of wool are made lustrous with an application of *hydrate of caustic soda,* and *formic acid* has also been used for this purpose.

PLEASE NOTE that many of these chemicals are dangerous and should never be used without knowledge of their properties and of the precautions needed when handling them.

Left:
Warp-printed silk, blistered by chemical treatment. 1935/6. Probably Bianchini Ferier, France. (Victoria and Albert Musuem, London: T416-1980)
Below:
Cotton check, discharge-printed after weaving. (Jeanette Killner, West Surrey College of Art and Design, UK)

Crimping
A soft form of pleating in which the cloth flutes instead of creases. Goffering irons, and other pleating devices, were used in homes at the turn of the century to maintain fluted and pleated trims after washing and starching.

Left:
Quadruple (tubular) scarf, cotton warp, wool weft. The very open sett is stabilized, and the cloth given bulk, during finishing when compression of the cloth produces crimping. (Junichi Arai, Japan)
Below:
Pleated linen fabric preserved in a bronze buckle. Excavated at Birka, Sweden. 9th century

1

1 Silk cloth designed to be pleated. (Anne Tomlin, West Surrey College of Art and Design, UK)
2 Silk scarf in which the weave is designed to create undulating folds after wet-finishing. 1988. (Ann Richards, UK)

Pleating
The process of folding cloth and pressing it into sharp creases dates back to the early Egyptians who used hot stones to make pleats in wet linen. More recently, industrial methods have looked for permanency in pleats by including some heat-sensitive fibres in the fabric to be pleated, or by applying synthetic resins. There are two ways in which pleats are inserted today: cloth can be cut in garment shape and placed into a pleated paper pattern mould. Another mould is placed on top, and the whole is rolled into a cone, and hot-set in a curling-oven. When the pleats are needed in yardage fabric, the cloth is fed between two heated rollers, and blades insert the pleats simultaneously.

2

CONCLUSION

When an idea is connected logically and organically to a way
of realizing that idea, the result is a piece of work which has
integrity and harmony. The development of a point of view,
so critical in making work of value and individuality,
results from balancing idea, experience and influence.
This compendium of ideas (which can never, by its nature,
be complete) is an attempt to provide a starting point for
the weaver, who may then be encouraged to develop and
expand the thinking in a personal direction. Curiosity,
investigation, rule-breaking and lateral thinking are the
foundations of creativity. If the future of the woven textile is
to be as exciting as its past, these aspects of its creation must
be given as much attention as, if not more attention than,
fine craftsmanship.

FURTHER READING

CREATIVITY AND PRE-WEAVING

Albers, Anni. *On Designing*. Middletown, CT: Wesleyan University Press, 1971.

De Bono, Edward. *The Use of Lateral Thinking*. London: Cape, 1964.

McKim, Robert. *Thinking Visually: A Strategy Manual for Problem-Solving*. Belmont, CA: Lifetime Learning Publications, 1980.

Rothenberg, Albert and Carl R. Hausman (eds). *The Creativity Question*. Durham, NC: Duke University Press, 1976.

Ward, Michael. *Art and Design in Textiles*. New York and London: Von Nostrand Reinhold, 1973.

INVENTION AND PROCESS

Fibres
Hearle, J.W.S. et al. *Structural Mechanics of Fibers, Yarns and Fabrics Vol. 1*. New York and London: Wiley Interscience, 1969.

Kornreich, E. *Introduction to Fibres and Fabrics: Their Manufacture and Properties*. London: Heywood Books; New York: American Elsevier Publishing Co., 1952.

Silk and Rayon Users' Association, The. *The Silk Book*. London, 1951.

Colour
Beaumont, Roberts, MSc, MI, MechE. *Colour in Woven Design*. London and New York: Whitaker, 1912.

Chevreul, M. E. *Chevreul on Colour: The Principles of Harmony and Contrast of Colours and their Applications to the Arts* (Translated by Charles Martel). London: George Bell and Sons, 1883.

De Grandis, Luigina. *Theory and Use of Color*. New York: Harry N. Abrams, 1986.

Lambert, Patricia et al. *Color and Fiber*. West Chester, PA: Schiffler, 1986.

Vincent, Sally and Jennie Crowder. *The New Dyer*. Loveland, CO: Interweave Press, 1981.

The Loom
Diderot, Denis. *Pictorial Encyclopedia of Science, Art, and Technology* (first published between 1751-1777). New York: Readex Microprint Corporation, 1969. Also republished (illustrations only) New York: Harry N. Abrams, 1978.

Fox, Thomas W. *The Mechanism of Weaving*. London: Macmillan, 1900, 1932.

Gilroy, Clinton C. *The Art of Weaving (by Hand and by Power)*. London: Wiley and Putnam, 1845.

Murphy, William S. *The Textile Industries – a Practical Guide* (8 vols). London: Gresham, 1845, 1911.

Ponting, Kenneth G. *Leonardo Da Vinci: Drawings for Textile Machines:* Wiltshire: Moonraker Press; NJ: Humanities Press, Pasold Research Fund Ltd, 1979.

Weaving and Finishing Processes
Barlow, Alfred. *The History and Principles of Weaving*. London: Sampson Low, Manston, Searle and Rivington, 1879.

Geiger, Agnes. *A History of Textile Art*. Pasold Research Fund/Sotheby Parke Bernet, 1979.

Gilonne, Georges et al. *Soiries de Lyons*. Editions du Fleuve, 1948.

Hollen, Norma and Jane Saddler. *Textiles*. New York and London: Macmillan, 1955, 1964.

Hooper, Luther. *Handloom Weaving*. New York: Pitman Publishing Ltd., Taplinger Publising Co., 1910.

Rowe, Ann Pollard. 'Interlocking Warp and Weft in the Nasca 2 Style', *Textile Museum Journal* (Washington, DC), December 1982.

Strong, John H. *Fabric Structure*. Brooklyn, New York: Chemical Publishing Co., 1947.

Weibel, Adele Coulin. *Two Thousand Years of Textiles*. New York: Pantheon Books/Detroit Institute of Arts, 1952.

Wingate, Isabel. *Textile Fabrics*. Engelwood Cliffs, NJ: Prentice-Hall, 1935, 1947.

INDEX